'Cummoangetaff!'

'Cummoangetaff!'

The Adventures of Big Aggie MacDonald,
the Glasgow Tramcar Clippie

ALLAN MORRISON

ILLUSTRATED BY

Besley

www.vitalspark.co.uk

Vital Spark is an imprint of
Neil Wilson Publishing Ltd
G/R 19 Netherton Avenue
Glasgow G13 1BQ
Tel: 0141-954-8007
Fax: 0560-150-4806
E-mail: info@nwp.co.uk
www.nwp.co.uk

Produced in association with
Waverley Books
144 Port Dundas Road
Glasgow G4 0HZ
Tel: 0141 567 2830
Fax: 0141 567 3831
E-mail: info@waverley-books.co.uk
www.waverley-books.co.uk

First printed in 2001
Reprinted 2002, 2005, 2010

With grateful thanks to Ion Campbell, Tom Dale,
Dr Neil A Mackillop, Andrew Pearson and Archie Wilson.

A catalogue record for this book is
available from the British Library.

ISBN 978-1-903238-31-8

Typeset in Bodoni
Designed by Mark Blackadder
Printed and bound in Poland

Contents

Preface   vii

1. Introducing Big Aggie MacDonald   1

2. The Story of the 'Shooglies'   7
   Tramlines   16

3. Big Aggie and the Great Race   25
   Tramlines   31

4. Big Aggie and the Bank Robbers   37
   Tramlines   41

5. Big Aggie and The Wedding   47
   Tramlines   53

6. Big Aggie has an Admirer   59
   Tramlines   62

7. Big Aggie and the Baby   69
   Tramlines   72

8. Big Aggie and The Cowboys   79
   Tramlines ... The End of the Line   82

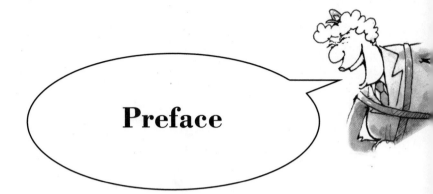

Preface

THESE STORIES OF Big Aggie MacDonald, the Glasgow tram conductress with the caustic wisecracking tongue, will take you back to the golden age of the tram. Her rich, biting patter, indiscriminately targeted at all and sundry, is the stuff for which streetwise Glaswegians have become renowned. In Aggie's day a hurl on a tramcar wasn't just another journey down to the shops – it was also a jaunt in an atmosphere of a constantly changing patois emanating from the likes of Big Aggie.

Nowadays we commute in the comfort of modern rolling stock on the railways and roads, frequently only pausing to place our 'precise fare' in the ticket machine or be handed a ticket from the cheerless conductor. It was never thus in Aggie's day when anyone with an opinion was likely to vent it between stops at anyone who was in earshot.

Tram travel was a fundamental part of life for the best part of 90 years in Glasgow. The city's trams were the most famous in the world, symbolising the city as much as shipbuilding and commerce. People spoke to one another on the trams. Wee drunk men were forever entertaining their fellow passengers with a song, a joke and a bit of banter. Folk passed round their chips and sweeties. And above all, people met, relationships were formed and many Glaswegians fell in love.

On a dark, wet, miserable night the trams were a haven of reassuring comfort as they shoogled Glaswegians homewards. And when the travellers finally reached home there was always a smile on their face as they recalled a joke, an aside or some of the magical patter between the likes of Big Aggie and her passengers!

CHAPTER 1
Introducing Big Aggie MacDonald

REMEMBER THE CLANK and rattle of the Glasgow trams, or 'caurs' as some folks called them? They always seemed to be full inside and up-top too: people squeezed together, cheek-by-jowl, with the platform and running-board full. Whenever it stopped, the conductress' voice rang out loud and clear, 'Cummoangetaff!' Then, once the alighting passengers had disembarked and others boarded, the same unmistakable demanding tone was heard. 'Right youse! Move right doon the caur! Ferrs, pal-leeze!'

Close your eyes and you can hear those wonderful sounds of yesteryear ... the beat of the wheels as the trams' bogies clattered over the many junctions, the squealing wheelflanges and the swishing of the collector on the overhead wire, together with the shrill voice of the

Move right doon the caur!

conductress (better known as the clippie) and her famous dictum, 'Cummoangetaff!'

To those uninitiated in the local vernacular, 'cummoangetaff!', simply translates as, 'come on, get off.' This has confused thousands of would-be English speakers and tourists to Scotland over the years, as they struggled to grasp the subtleties of Scottish communication, intermingled with its rich, biting humour. 'Come on ...' is an encouragement to the passenger to move quickly; '... get aff' translates as, 'Get off this tram as there is a queue of folk waiting to get on, and we have a timetable to keep to!'

The swaying coloured trams, sometimes referred to as 'shooglies', dominated the busy pulsating City of Glasgow until 1962. Trams revolutionised city life and travel. They made it possible for workers to live in the suburbs, justified the building of power stations, and the flexibility of transport helped relieve unemployment.

Glasgow belonged to the trams and the trams to Glasgow as John Price, the tramway historian, recorded. 'The immortal Standard Tramcar is typically Glaswegian. Fifty years old, all dark wood and brass fittings and blue pipe-smoke in the upper saloon, rolling home with a slightly inebriated four-wheel motion that belongs to Will Fyfe's Glasgow as surely do the late night crowds singing upstairs. Half-a-century hard at work, bruised, battered and patched.'

When, during the First World War, more than 3,000 Glasgow tram personnel left to fight in France, women were recruited as both conductresses and motormen, i.e. the drivers. For almost the next 50 years these ladies made their mark on Glasgow culture, for the trams seemed to spawn a unique breed of person.

PIPE SMOKE IN THE UPPER SALOON

2

Do you recall the verses from the poem, The Glasgow Lament?

And where is the tram car that once did a ton
Doon the Great Western Road on the old Yoker run?
The conductress aye knew how to deal wi' the nyaff,
'If yer gaun, then get oan, if yer no' then get aff!'

The tram's squeelin' wheelflanges aye made a great fuss,
Wi' weird clickin' noises no' found on a bus,
The conductress wis cheeky an' fu' o' the chaff,
Shoutin', 'Hurry up, mister, Cummoangetaff!'

'Move doon the caur noo, there's plenty o' room,
You'll aw get a seat afore we hit toon,
Nae smokin' doon here, pal, only up tap,
Pit oot that fag, haud oan tae yer strap!'

Fae Dalmuir an' Barrheid way oot tae the west,
Tae Airdrie and Uddingston as good as the rest.
Passengers fae Clydebank or tough Govan men,
Folks from oot Riddrie and old Rutherglen.

They aw used the trams, it is a dead shame,
The caurs are awa', but left is their fame.
Ah fair miss the clippies, aw hard as nails,
An' the pennies ah bent oan the auld tramway rails.

Ah think o' these days o' ma tenement hame,
We've noo fancy hooses, but they're no' jist the same,
Ah'll swop yer gizunders, flyovers and jams,
Fur a tuppenny ride on an auld Glesca tram.

Anon.

The conductress on board these old tramcars was probably our heroine, Big Aggie MacDonald!

Glasgow had many well-known tram clippies, Maggie MacDougall from Auchenshuggle and Bridie McPherson, but Big Aggie MacDonald was IT! The 'big-yin', the doyen of them all: a

3

monumental, self-assured extrovert, she was put on this earth for the sole purpose of dealing with cheeky weans, fare dodgers, drunks, nyaffs, self-righteous wee wummen from Milngavie or those who lived up 'half-tiled' wally closes and drank tea with raised pinkies. Big Aggie had a talent for pricking pomposity while simultaneously delivering a line in self-deprecation. Any Glasgwegian jouking on or off her tram without a ticket got a rude awakening with her ribald comments, for nobody stole a hurl on Aggie's caur.

'those who drank tea with raised pinkies...'

Her regular motorman was Jimmy Tamson. She never could remember his name properly, but knew that as he came from Glasgow it had to be Jimmy! Jimmy depended on Aggie for back up when a problem was encountered, and so readily forgave her her many eccentricities. Indeed, in his local of an evening, he could be relied on to recount the latest adventures of a day spent working with Big Aggie.

But Aggie had an enemy, Corporation Tram Inspector Colin Campbell. (After the Second World war tram inspectors were referred to as the 'Gestapo' by staff.) He was a proud Highlander, and one who was continually at war with any MacDonald, especially Big Aggie. Campbell was small of stature, thus putting him at an immediate disadvantage to Big Aggie. His sole ambition in life seemed to be to find fault with Aggie's duties. Conductresses could be suspended for failing to have a clean bottle-green uniform, or having buttons and badges unpolished, or indeed – the worst crime of all – allowing passengers to stand on the top deck. Despite some near things, Wee Campbell usually came off second best to Aggie.

Inspector Campbell

The tramlines may have gone but the trams are cherished in the memory of millions of Scots. Clippies like Big Aggie MacDonald remain in the psyche. She, in keeping with hundreds of others, was a domineering matriarch of all she surveyed on her

4

tram, shoogling to all parts of Glasgow and its outlying districts.

Cummoangetaff! captures the robust, irreverent humour and one-liners, all in the famous Glasgow patois, with which Big Aggie ruled the roost, displaying her total abhorrence of pretension. Aggie did not 'miss and hit the wall!' Head-on, she coped with situations which would certainly have brought lesser mortals to their knees. The motto of the Transport Department of Glasgow was, *'Safety, Courtesy and Efficiency'*. Big Aggie MacDonald was certainly hot on safety and efficiency!

Aggie worked on most of the routes; the number 26 from Burnside to Scotstoun, the number 22 from Lambhill to Possilpark and the number 9 from Auchenshuggle to Dalmuir West, amongst many others. Major thoroughfares like Argyle Street belonged to the tram. From early morning until the late evening, they bustled along; singly at times but in convoys as often as not – like a conquering armada. And every tram running through Argyle Street (and, it should be said, Princes Street in Edinburgh and Union Street in Aberdeen, too) was dominated by an imposing conductress like Aggie.

Cummoangetaff! brings all those wonderful memories back from the **golden age of the tram.**

CHAPTER 2
The Story
of the 'Shooglies'

THE GLASGOW TRAMS are remembered sentimentally, not just by Glaswegians, but by all Scots. The Glasgow 'caurs' seemed to have had a magic all of their very own.

However, as the trams in Glasgow ceased running in 1962, some people today may have no real idea what a tramcar was. It has been described as a 'high-built glittering galleon of the streets'. Certainly in some respects this is a good description. It had two decks, railing around the top one, bulkheads, a fog bell, and sticking out of the top was not a funnel or a sail, but a current collector (bow collector). The driver (or motorman) used two brass handles. One, the controller for

'GALLEON OF THE STREETS'

setting the tram in motion using the electric power, the other a brake. Trams did not turn around when they got to their destination. At the terminus the conductress or conductor merely flipped over the backrests of the bench seats like a set of dominoes. Destination boards were at both ends of a tram so what had just been the back of the vehicle became the front. It was also necessary to swing the bow collector around. This current collector swivelled on the roof of the tram, sloping skyward, pressing against the electrical cables above.

The trams in Britain are attributed to an American, surprisingly called George Train. Train had travelled the world and it is said he was the inspiration for Jules Verne's *Around the World in Eighty Days*. In his home town of Philadelphia he had observed coaches with flanged wheels running on tracks which, although drawn by two horses, could carry 60 passengers compared with the normal 20.

George Train formed a company and the first British tram ran in Birkenhead in 1860. In 1870 Parliament passed 'The Tramway Act' by which Town Councils could own tramlines though the running of the trams had to be by private companies. However the councils could take them over after they had been running for 21 years. The tramway began in Glasgow when the first horse-drawn trams, seating 40 passengers, came into existence on the 19th August 1872. The inaugural service was between St George's Cross and Eglington Toll, a distance of just over two miles. Seven tartan-liveried trams were each hauled by two horses at a top speed of 10mph. They were operated by Andrew Menzies, the bus operator.

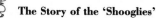

The trams were heavy, and it was not unusual to see a horse stumble and go down on slippery or frosty cobbles. The routine then was that the driver sat on the horse's head, talking to it to calm the animal down, while the conductor unhitched the beast. Then a hood would be put over its head until it got to its feet again. Those horse-drawn trams were sometimes followed by gangs of wee boys with buckets and shovels, keen to collect manure to sell to Glasgow citizens with gardens.

In 1878, steam-powered trams were run in the south of the city by the Vale of Clyde Tramways. The fare was $^1/_2$p on the open top and 1p inside. People would sit on the top deck with their gamp up in inclement weather. On very wet days straw was put on the floor of the top deck.

The whole tramway system expanded until in 1894, the total length of track was over 31 miles. The gauge between the rails was 4ft $7^3/_4$in (1.42m), in order that railway wagons could run on flanges in the groove of the rail. The tram rails were set into smooth grey cobbles. As the tall glass-sided vehicles moved sedately along, their wheels grated on the metal rails with a sonorous note that reverberated from tenement walls.

The trams were owned and operated by the Glasgow Tramway and Omnibus Company Limited. However Glasgow Corporation, seeing the popularity of the tram system, opted to take it over after the 21-year lease expired. The Glasgow Tramway and Omnibus Company refused to participate in the would-be takeover, and wouldn't hand over any of its rolling stock or equipment. So the city fathers had to create a new fleet of cars, plant, stables, horses and ancillary equipment.

On the 30th June 1894, Glasgow Corporation became the first British city to own and operate its own public transport system. The first corporation tram left the Dalmarnock depot on the 1st July. At that time they had 384 horse-drawn trams, 3,000 horses, 9 depots and 31 miles of track. The conditions of the drivers and conductors were improved

Standard

Coronation

by five hours less work to a 10-hour day. The weekly pay went from 21 shillings to 25 shillings. Between 1898 and 1902 the system was changed over to electric traction. The total cost of the electrification project was half-a-million pounds. Electricity for the entire tramway system was generated by a new power station at Pinkston.

The first 21 electric trams were American style single-deckers, referred to by Glaswegians, because of their limited space, as 'room and kitchen caurs'. One hundred and twenty horse-drawn trams were converted to electricity. The first of the familiar four-wheeled 'Standard' models came in 1898/99. More than one thousand were eventually built, many of them to survive in service for over 50 years. They could seat 59 passengers, 21 below, 38 above. Their length overall was 28ft (8.53m), the height 15ft 8in (4.77m), and with a breadth of 7ft 2in (2.19m).

Around 1930 the fleet of Standard trams were rebuilt to increase speed, comfort and safety. Upholstery replaced the wooden seats and the top deck balconies were enclosed. New motors increased the maximum service speed to around 28mph (45kph). It is interesting to note that on the old Standards it was the conductresses' responsibility, when the tram was turning left, to be on the rear platform with arm extended.

In 1936 a new style of Glasgow tram appeared with the 'Coronation'. They were built at the Coplawhill works at a cost of £4,406 each. The Coronation was 34ft long (10.36m), 7ft 3½in wide (2.22m), and 15ft 8½in high (4.79m). Twenty-seven passengers could be seated inside in the saloon and 38 upstairs.

A major innovation was the provision of a separate driving cabin, with a door and a seat. The old Standard had a wooden portholed bulkhead door as the only division between the motorman and passengers, held open to give a cooling breeze on hot days by the 'auld poker', the point-iron, used to change the points on the rails at complex junctions. The driver of a Coronation also had a new range of equipment to help him or her, including dipping headlights, a sunshade, separate stop and fog lights, trafficator lights on each side of the dash and a retractable mirror. Below the cab was a steel collision

Cunarder

fender carrying a drawbar coupling. The concealed lighting inside was fitted with moulded shades and extended the whole length of the saloon. The upper saloon ceiling was treated to resist nicotine stains. The livery was orange on the lower deck and the upper deck in 'bus green'. The ivory of the relieving lines along the tram sides was carried round the dash plates in a downswept 'V' above maroon fenders and bogies.

Points policemen in Glasgow could stand between passing Standard trams due to the old trams' narrowing waists. However when in 1948 a mark II Coronation was introduced, named the Cunarder, this was no longer possible due to their increased breadth. The Cunarder did not have some of the more decorative refinements of the Coronation. For example the lighting was simplified and the ducted air ventilation was dispensed with in favour of sliding windows. The lower saloon held 30 or 26 depending on the seat configuration and the upper deck 40. However the travelling public were never

SPAM CAN

happy with the three steps up to the interior and its cramped seating. Also their 'tinny' sounding bogies gave rise to them being referred to as 'Spam cans'!

Timetables had to be strictly adhered to. Drivers were required to clock-in at clocks, called a 'Bundy', at the side of selected streets en route. Strict rules for the public were established for travelling on trams, with notices scattered around both the upper and lower decks.

Spitting strictly forbidden, penalty forty shillings.

(This notice gave rise to the Glasgow children's limerick:

There was an old man from Darjeeling,
Who sat with an orange he was peeling,
It said on the door,
Don't spit on the floor,
So he carefully spat on the ceiling.)

Please face direction car is travelling.

10 standing passengers are permitted in the lower saloon when all seats are occupied on the vehicle.

(Some notices concluded with: There is no restriction to the number of standing passengers on the LAST TRAM on any route.)

The Transport Dept. is not responsible for passengers' luggage.

Caution: Don't go round the back of this vehicle on leaving.

No standing on the platform.

No wonder conductresses became authoritative in order to enforce the rules, control crowds and take fares.

In the early days of the trams, colours denoted the different routes, rather than numbers, as many people could not read. One wonders how they read the instruction notices inside the trams? Tram stop signs varied. Some simply said, *Tram Stop*, others *Fare Stage*, *All Trams Stop Here*, and some *Cars Stop Here If Required*. The colouring system continued and many routes were referred to, for example, as 'yellow caur' or perhaps 'red caur' routes. It was almost like today's postal code system. Couthy Glaswegians would talk about those considered to have 'a bool in their mooths' as 'having a yellow caur accent.'

Red honesty boxes, referred to as the 'wee red box', were placed on the platforms, in which passengers were supposed to place uncollected fares on alighting. This was not popular with conductresses, as it was felt that too much money in the box reflected badly on their efficiency. Sometimes in frosty weather the trams would jump the rails and the driver had to reverse a bit and try again using the 'auld-poker' at the points. Dried sand was also provided to drivers in order that it could be applied to rails on gradients in very wet conditions. At very busy junctions sometimes a 'points-boy' was employed to change the points.

An extraordinary comradeship existed between tramway employees. This was demonstrated by an entire Highland Light Infantry, City of Glasgow Regiment, (Tramways Battalion), being recruited during the First World War. On March 17th, 1941, during German bombing, tramcar number 6 was destroyed in Nelson Street, with a number of fatalities. During this time of bombing tram services were limited in the city. Many tram windows were blown out with bomb blasts and were replaced with opaque glass. In 1943 a number of the longer routes were cut to minimize delays caused by ever increasing breakdowns. Unfortunately breakdowns and even derailments grew common, and on the 9th August 1944 a major power failure at the Pinkston Station resulted in police having to be called in to disperse queues of angry passengers in Argyle Street.

The Golden Jubilee of the trams was on the 1st July 1944, by which time there were 1,207 trams and 135 miles of track. By 1948, 85% of the trams were at least 35 years old and with the ever improving bus service, and the growing number of private cars, the days of the 'caurs' were numbered.

In February 1949 the trams got a further rival – the trolley-bus. The first delivery of these vehicles amounted to 64. However they were fraught with problems. The biggest difficulty for the trolley-bus driver was keeping the trolleys, or 'booms' as they were called, on the overhead wires. There were also 'dead' sections of wire wherever there were intersections and these had to be coasted without the aid of power. The turn from St Vincent Street into West Nile Street was notoriously difficult. The trolley-buses only lasted 18 years. In 1954 the last six trams were built for the Glasgow fleet (numbers 1393-1398). They were of 'Coronation' design.

On the 4th September 1962, a crowd of 230,000 people turned out in pouring rain to say farewell to this transport legend. The Number 9 from Dalmuir West to Auchenshuggle was the final tram. However, although this was the date of the last official run, the corporation kept some trams going for three more days to give the adoring public the chance of a final shoogle.

These people, along with millions of other Scots spread throughout the world, would never forget the characteristic shape, colour, noise and smell of these dignified goddesses. They still remember the clatter of the destination blind being changed at the terminus, the staccato clatter as seat backs were swung over, the stained glass at the top of the windows, the platform bell and the driver's brass handles. And how, at night, as the tram moved along the wire, the pole made a sizzling sound with a magical, blue, tracery of flying sparks at tight junctions. The deep sense of loss of the Glasgow trams prevails to this very day.

But the trams are not dead! Britain has the line between Blackpool and Fleetwood; South Yorkshire has trams and of course

LAST TRAM TO
AUCHENSHUGGLE

there is the Metrolink in Manchester. Most European cities wisely retained their tramways and some American cities have them. Edinburgh is again considering trams to solve city congestion. Trams have a lasting fascination. For conveying large numbers of people around a city they have yet to be surpassed. The author (a Glaswegian of course!) believes that it is only a matter of time before Glasgow realizes its dreadful mistake and brings back the 'caurs'. Then, no doubt, the descendants of Big Aggie MacDonald and her ilk will ensure that once more the old city again will hear that lyrical cry ... 'CUMMOANGETAFF!'

TRAMLINES

The everyday tales of Glasgow tram conductress, Big Aggie MacDonald, and her reputed altercations with the travelling public.

✳   ✳   ✳

The Number 15 tram at Glasgow Cross was stappit fu' inside and up top, with people squeezed together, cheek-by-cheek; the platform and running board full. The caur stopped, and Aggie seeing a massive queue shouted, 'Room for wan only!'

The middle-aged, rather prim and proper couple at the head of the line stepped forward. The rotund wife protested. 'Come on, my dear, surely ye wouldnae separate a man from his wife?'

'Yer right,' exclaimed Aggie with a compassionate smile, rang the bell, and off went the caur ... leaving the queue intact.

The French visitors to the city looked on blankly as Big Aggie shouted out instructions to the queue of people on Argyle Street waiting to board her tram.

'If them that's cumin' oan'll get aff, them that's gettin' aff'll get oan better!'

* * *

There was a build up of traffic ahead, and the number 18 tram had been stationary for almost five minutes at the junction of Union Street and Argyle Street.

A voice addressed Aggie from within the lower saloon. 'Hey, hen. Whit's haudin' up yer driver? We've been sittin' here fur dunkeys.'

Aggie's rasping reply rang out loud and clear. 'Well, you'll just need tae keep sittin' oan yer asses, fur there urnae oany dunkeys!'

* * *

Aggie's bosom was of enormous size, a bruiser of a chest upholstered in serge-green corporation uniform, and perhaps the reason she had acquired the description of 'big'. As it thundered towards you at full tilt, you got the feeling that here was a heaving mass from which there could be no escape. Her persona and shape emitted a clear message – 'Wha' daur meddle wi' me!' The answer was damn few, unless fuelled by strong drink.

'You've goat a rare big boady oan ye, Aggie,' observed one gent, clearly the worse of drink, as he eyed up Aggie's ample bosom.

'Did ye work oot wi' dumbells at school?'

'Why? Whit school wur ye in?'

* * *

'In aw yer time oan the caurs, have ye ever had an accident, Aggie?' asked a regular on the number 14 to Kelvingrove.

'Nut one,' replied Aggie emphatically.

'Ah wid o' thought it could be a right dangerous joab, especially oan a Saturday night.'

'Well,' admitted Aggie. 'Ah've been hit o'er the heid wi' a handbag, had a bag o' chips tossed at me, an' ma ankle nipped by a wee dug.'

'An' ye don't call these accidents?'

'Nut on yer life. The buggers did it on purpose!'

* * *

The man jumped on Aggie's tram at the corner of Hope Street and Sauchiehall Street. He was halfway up the stairs before she bawled. 'An' where the hell dae ye think yer goin'?'

'Up the sterrs. Are there nae seats?'

'There's thirty-eight o' them.'

'Great,' responded the passenger and moved again to climb the stairs.

'Ah said,' repeated Aggie's rasping voice, 'an' where the hell dae ye think yer goin'?'

'Tae get a seat up the sterr.'

'They've aw goat bums oan them!'

The sad, elderly gentleman wearing an old tile hat, held a sign proclaiming, 'The End is Nigh'. He sat on the inside seat, near the rear platform, on Aggie's tram.

　　With downcast eyes he addressed her. 'My dear, who are we? What is the meaning of life? Where are we going?'

　　'An OAP, God knows, and Partick Cross!'

*　　*　　*

The number 18 to Springburn was behind schedule, and a man with a wooden leg was holding up the queue as he attempted the stairs to the upper deck. Big Aggie immediately shouted out.

　　'Folks wi' two legs up tap – folks wi' wan leg inside!'

*　　*　　*

'Dae ye go tae the university, Missis?' asked an innocent young student passenger.

　　'Naw, son. Ah'm just a caur conductress.'

*　　*　　*

The queue at Partick Cross was huge but the tram was almost full. Big Aggie standing on the rear platform roared, 'Wan only!'

　　At the head of the queue was a Glasgow worthy and his greyhound. As he stepped forward to mount the platform Aggie moved forward. 'Ah said wan only!'

　　'But it's only a dug.'

　　'You can get oan, or yer dug. Naw both!'

　　'Well, nane o' us will get oan in that case!'

　　A lady, second in the queue, moved onto the tram, Aggie rang the bell and off went the caur. The man with the greyhound shouted after Aggie. 'Away an' stuff yer tram up yer jumper!'

　　Aggie yelled back. 'Aye, an' if you'd stuffed yer dug up yer jumper ye'd baith huv goat oan!'

19

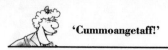
* * *

The lady of easy virtue sat upstairs smoking. She wore bleached hair falling in crimped waves beyond her shoulders, had a tiny nose and a large pouting mouth. Her eyes were deep-set and dark.

She had finished selling her charms for the night, and managed to catch Big Aggie's late-night tram home.

'That you away hame, hen, tae get a bed tae yersel', then?' was Aggie's observation as she collected her fare.

* * *

It was Christmas and the tramcar was held up by a marching Salvation Army band at Glasgow Cross.

'Whit's yer favourite hymn, Aggie?' ventured a regular passenger.

'Him wi' that big drum!'

* * *

The young man who had just come on board looked around for the conductress.

'Hey! Do you know that the front destination board on this tram says it's a 15 to Baillieston but it has number 32 on the side,' he remarked with a smug grin.

'Well, let me tell you something, Mister Smart Erse,' replied Aggie. 'This tram is goin' furrit, no' sidywize!'

* * *

The first dozen or so passengers got onboard the tram at George Square before Aggie sprang forward on the rear platform, arm outstretched, barring the way to any others. 'That's it. We ur full!' she announced.

The man now at the head of the queue shouted back at her in an annoyed tone. 'Hey you! How lang will the next tram be?'

Aggie drew herself up to her full height, and looking him straight in the eye, rasped. 'The same length as this wan!'

*   *   *

Big Aggie was collecting fares on the top deck of an 18A to Shawfield. 'Where did you board the caur?' she demanded of one sullen youth who had just drawn a soaken sleeve across his snotty nose and stuck his tongue out at her.

'Doonstairs.'

'Aye. An' that's where yer getting aff, right noo. Cummoangetaff! Aff, O–F–F, aff!'

*   *   *

The morning caur was caught in the rush-hour traffic of Argyle Street. Many of the frustrated passengers anxiously looked at their watches.

Big Aggie came down the stairs, happily whistling.

'Hey, Aggie. Whit are you so happy aboot? We're aw late,' moaned a wee man in a bowler hat.

'Ah'm already at ma work!' replied Aggie.

*   *   *

'Ferrs, pal-leeze! Noo, where are ye going, mister?' asked Big Aggie.

'Ah'm going tae ma first wife's fur ma tea.'

'Can the new wan no' cook, then?'

*   *   *

'I must get home to prepare my good man's tea, conductress. You know, time has simply flown while I was in Lewis's store choosing my hat,' remarked one well-dressed lady to Aggie.

'Well,' observed Aggie. 'If you'd as many feathers stickin' oot yer erse as ye hiv in yer hat, ye could've flown hame!'

*   *   *

A passenger was anxiously watching her baggage as it sat in the wee space under the stairs, beneath a notice which said, '*WARNING. The Transport Department. is not responsible for passengers' luggage.*'

'Are you sure it's safe there?' she asked Aggie.

'Listen, hen, ah'm like the Govan polis. Never loast a case yet!'

✳   ✳   ✳

The very tall lad on the number 15 to Anderston Cross produced tuppence. 'Half-fare, missis.'

'An' how old ur ye, sunshine?' demanded Aggie.

'Fifteen.'

'Oh, aye! An' when will ye be sixteen?'

'When ah get aff this tram,' came the cheeky reply.

'Well, aff! O–F–F, aff … and by the way … happy birthday!'

✳   ✳   ✳

One day Aggie was overheard shouting to a passenger who was slow to respond. 'Did ye hear me? Dae ye want a fourpenny ticket tae Giffnock? Gies an answer!'

'Ah did. Ah shook ma heid.'

'Well ye didna expect me tae hear it rattle wi' aw the noise aff the caur, did ye?'

✳   ✳   ✳

The rather large woman was out of breath as she stepped onto the platform of the tram going into town.

'Do you know, conductress,' she exclaimed. 'A've run fifty yards tae catch this tram.'

'Aye, well ye'd better talk tae ma driver,' replied Aggie. 'He's the wan who's givin' oot the prizes!'

'How lang have ye been on the caurs noo, Aggie?' enquired one of her regular passengers. 'An' before that did ye have a war record?'

'Hey, that's two questions. Twenty years and three by Vera Lynn.'

'Ferrs, pal-leeze!' demanded Aggie as she made her way up the swaying lower deck of a Coronation number 29 to Tollcross. As she did so her left hand jingled a pile of pennies ready for change.

The well-dressed lady looked up at her, money in hand, and replied in a somewhat superior way, 'I'm swithering.'

'Wur no' goin' there. There's nae rails!'

Aggie's tram, a number 31, had reached the Lambhill terminus.

'Right!' shouted Aggie. 'Here we are fur where we're goin'. Aw them that's here fur there, get aff!'

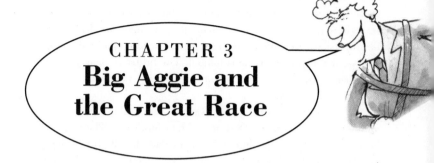

CHAPTER 3
Big Aggie and the Great Race

BIG AGGIE MACDONALD'S hands were impressive. Disproportionately large, they had proved capable on many occasions (as the reader will shortly learn) of punching more than a ticket.

Aggie seemed impervious to all attacks; no passenger ever considered making a grab for her cash-bag. Indeed her thick fingers, which gave evidence to a high dependency on Craven A, the cigarettes she favoured, would have throttled anyone who tried.

Aggie was also high-rumped, with wide hips and matching thighs, victims of a penchant for fish and pie suppers. But the eyes were what immediately caught the observer. Composed, they carried the weight of distinct intellect and wisdom. The formidable steely glint immediately warned off any citizen considering anything other than paying the correct fare.

An apparent genius at mathematics, she knew intimately the fare structure between any two points on the tram network. However, on occasion, when faced with a passenger whom she considered warranted compassion, Big Aggie was known to construct her own unique charging system.

Aggie had a soft spot for her regular driver, Jimmy Tamson. Her loyalty to him was legendary. His problems were her problems, and nothing illustrated this more than the 'Great Race', as it has now come to be known.

It took place at the time when Big Aggie and Jimmy were on the Renfrew to Keppochill route, during the winter of 1951/52. A few of the tram drivers and conductors on that route had just retired, and the duo were filling in for three months.

Really the drama all started in the Renfrew Arms public bar one Saturday lunchtime. Twister Jack, a bus driver of some notoriety, stood, his arms plunged elbow-deep inside the waistband of his uniform trousers. His back against a bar stanchion, he was busy scratching at some hidden, annoying itch. Seeing tram drivers in the bar, his beady eyes filled with cunning and he said in a loud voice, 'Of course, the day o' the tram is limited. The future is clearly the bus.' He turned, winked at the barman and raised the pint to his half-smiling lips, waiting.

It didn't take long. Jimmy Tamson just couldn't resist the bait about his beloved trams. 'Nut at all,' he countered. 'The trams have been around fur mair than fifty years and they'll still be here in another fifty. They're immortal. Buses are smelly, unreliable things. Anyway, passengers like the trams.'

'Yer wrong, Jimmy,' retorted Twister, now peering at him over the rim of his glass. 'Your tram shoogles aboot like a Clyde steamer in a gale. The buses are comfortable. They're flexible. They can go anywhere. Anyhow, they're much faster than trams that wis built at the turn o' the century.'

'Faster! Listen you! Ma tram might be gettin' oan a bit but it wid beat your bus oany day. Ah can get up quite a turn o' speed, ye know.' A nerve twitched rhythmically next to Jimmy's right eye.

'Dinna be silly, man,' came Twister's voice. 'Yer auld tram widnae hae oany chance against ma bus in a race.'

It was only afterwards that Jimmy regretted his second hauf-and-a-hauf for he heard himself say. 'If ye want a race, I'll gie ye wan.'

Twister's face screwed up in thought. 'Tell ye what, Jimmy. I'll bet ye a pound ma bus will beat your tram, anytime, anywhere. We're oan much the same route. Jist you pick the time an' I'll be there. Here's ma haun oan the bet – but only if you're up tae it, mind you.'

'An' here's mine,' came Jimmy, impulsively adding, 'Why don't we make it a fiver?' and shoved a sweaty palm into the cool grip of the bus driver. Twister kept a firm grasp of Jimmy's hand and looked into the tram driver's face. 'Fine wi' me, Jimmy. Noo ye'll no' chicken oot and forget the whole thing, eh? Let's say it's goat tae be within the next month, or ah win.'

Jimmy's free hand clenched involuntarily. 'Within the next month, nae problem. Yer fiver's as good as mine.'

His hand released, Jimmy downed the remainder of his drinks, hauled on his peaked cap, and swaggered to the door.

It was in the cold air outside that the first feelings of regret came. A fiver was about his wages for the week. Everybody in the bar had heard the bet. Hadn't there been some laughter and sniggering in the background as he shook Twister's hand? He saw buses everyday zooming past his tram. He was in deep trouble.

During the next week Aggie could tell Jimmy was not himself. The pawky sense of humour and good-natured backchat had gone. Black patches appeared under his eyes. She wondered if he was ill.

One day at the terminus in Springburn, the seat backs had been quickly turned around and the current collector switched over. There were a few minutes before they started off. Jimmy sat, head down, picking away the remnants of cigarette paper from a pile of 'douts' he had collected. He disconsolately rubbed the shreds of tobacco together between his palms to form a 'makings', then, using a leaf of Rizla cigarette paper, rolled a fag. Aggie took the opportunity to raise her concern.

'Jimmy,' she quietly observed, 'when we wur going through Springburn the day, ah noticed wan o' they X-ray vans. You know, they test ye fur the TB. Mibbe ye should go?'

'Ah've no' goat TB,' came the adamant, downcast reply.

Aggie could stand it no longer. Jimmy wis the best driver in the depot and he wis her friend. It just had to be said.

'Well, see you, Jimmy, yer no' lookin' o'er healthy. November's a bad month for the flu and things. Ye should go an' see the doctor.'

There was a long silence followed by a number of sighs. He looked at the floor of the tram. It was time to tell Aggie his problem.

Out it came, all the details of the stupid bet, and finally the real problem. He couldn't afford to lose a fiver. His wife wouldnae half kill him. How could they feed the weans?

'Twister took ye fur a right mug there. It's diabolical ye took his bet. That's whit it is, diabolical!' But after a moment Aggie mused, 'Never mind Jimmy. A problem is better shared. Ah'll think aboot it.'

But think as she might it seemed Aggie too was stumped. She really needed help on this one.

It came in the form of a passenger the very next day. He had boarded at Renfrew Cross, a silver-haired man with a kindly smile. When Aggie asked him for his fare he produced a Corporation Gold staff pass. 'It makes a grand change to be sittin' in the back rather than drivin' this thing,' he commented.

'Don't tell me you're wan o' they folks we're replacin' at the minute?'

27

'Aye, ah'm just retired. It's a great feelin'. Dae whit ye like, an free hurls on the trams and buses. Ma name's Bob, by the way. Nice tae meet ye.' And he stood to shake Aggie's hand.

She introduced herself and thought. 'Whit a nice man. No' often ah get this courtesy fae tram drivers.'

Then it came to her. Maybe auld Bob could help with Jimmy's problem.

'Boab,' she ventured, 'can ah' ask ye a technical question? Could this tram go faster than a bus?'

'No way, Aggie. This is an old Standard, built in nineteen-canteen. Their top speed is twenty-eight miles per hour, though if it wis doon a steep gradient you might make forty. Corporation buses can dae over sixty, ah'm told.'

Aggie tightened her lips. It certainly wasn't the reply she had hoped for.

She thought for a minute, and then figured there was nothing to lose by telling him the problem.

When she finished he nodded his head and sympathised. 'Ah know that Twister Jack. He's aye up tae some nonsense.' The eyes blinked. He too was clearly thinking over the situation.

'There could be one way,' Bob volunteered. 'But ye'd need a bit o' good fortune. Here's whit ye might consider … '

Later at the terminus when she told Jimmy, his face lit up and he smiled for the first time in days.

'Aye, but remember, Jimmy. We'll need a pile o' luck,' added Aggie.

So it was that the following Saturday, Jimmy walked into the Renfrew Arms to be greeted by nudging smiles from Twister and his cronies.

'Only a fortnight tae go and ye'll owe me that fiver,' Twister exclaimed. 'Unless yer in tae tell me when and where the great race is.'

Jimmy smiled. He quietly ordered his hauf-and-a-hauf before turning to Twister and raising his voice. 'Well, ah wis thinkin, Jack, that as this is Renfrew the race should be near here.'

'Fine wi' me.'

'Whit aboot thon straight stretch from the foot of Glasgow Road to Hillington Road, wi' the winnin' post the turn-aff at Shieldhall. It's probably aboot a mile an' a hauf.'

'Ideal, Jimmy,' grinned Twister, who immediately thought, 'A straight stretch. Whit a mug. I'll be finished afore he's hauf nor quarter way there.' Then, putting his arm around Jimmy, he said. 'And here wis me thinking you would want tae forget all aboot oor bet, ma frien'.'

'Naw, naw, ah wis rememberin' it fine. Noo ah've tae pick the time tae, so it will be wan night during the next fortnight. Big Aggie an me get tae the foot o' Glasgow Road at 8.15 every night. Ah had a look at your timetable an it ties in perfect wi' oors on the same route.'

'Just you tell me which night, an' I'll be there ready,' said Twister, having real difficulty keeping the triumph off his face.

'Is it a' richt if I tell you oan the very day o' the race?'

Twister turned to his friends and winked. 'Nae problem. Just you decide, pal. You know me. Ah'm aw heart.'

The next few days were nail-biting for Jimmy and Aggie. In fact it was getting to the stage where Aggie had secretly determined she would pay half the bet if Jimmy lost. Efter aw, he had tae feed his weans, she reasoned.

Two days before the month's deadline ran out, Jimmy and Aggie met at the depot to clock in. Both gave a joyous whoop. Tonight would be perfect. The forecast on the wireless was dire.

When the tram got to Renfrew, Jimmy left the vehicle for a few minutes and nipped into the Arms.

Sure enough, there was Twister having a refreshment before his shift.

'Tonight's the race, everybody,' Jimmy announced in a loud voice.

Twister looked up. 'Ye canny be serious? It's a pee-souper oot there.'

'Anytime, any place. Remember?' replied Jimmy. 'Yer no' sayin' yer frightened o' a wee drap o' fog.'

The look on Twister's face was grim. He looked at his friends and realised there was no way out.

'We start at the foot o' Glasgow Road at 8.15,' reminded Jimmy.

'Ah'll be there. Dinnae ye worry.' But Twister's voice lacked enthusiasm.

At the allotted time, Standard tram number 44 stood at the fare stage at the beginning of the Hillington straight. It was almost full. Word had got around about the race.

Thick, yellow fog hung low, shrouding the road all around. The street lights vainly tried to pierce the enveloping swirls, as a crawling bus emerged from the gloom and stopped beside the tram. It was Twister. Only two passengers were onboard his vehicle.

Both drivers could just make out the figure of old Bob on the pavement holding a handkerchief aloft. Ahead, it was impossible to see more than six feet into the swirling mist. Bob's hand came down and the race was on.

Immediately Jimmy turned his brass handle to the maximum speed position. He quickly lost any sight of the bus as the tram hurtled blindly along the rails. Aggie stood directly behind Jimmy.

'Are ye sure auld Bob has got this right?' asked Jimmy anxiously.

'Don't you worry, Jimmy, Bob knows the route well.' Then a few moments later she shouted, 'One!' into his ear. The tram swayed alarmingly from side to side.

Thirty seconds later came her voice again. 'Two!'

It only seemed a short time before she was shouting again, 'Eight!' at which Jimmy brought his speed down to 10 miles an hour.

'Nine and stop!' Aggie finally yelled. There was a relieved cheer from the passengers inside.

The tram wheezed to a halt. Everyone peered into the yellow darkness. Sure enough, there, just beyond the front bogie, was the start of the turn-off to Shieldhall. The tram sat for five minutes, before a bus crept dejectedly out of the gloom behind them and drew alongside.

The red, angry face of Twister Jack could just be seen. He switched off his engine and jumped from his cab onto the road and shouted into Jimmy at the front of the tram. 'Ah'm no' payin' ye a penny. Ye cheated. Naebuddy could race on a night like this.'

The smile on Jimmy's face disappeared. 'You owe me a fiver. Ah won fair an square. Sure ah did, Aggie?' and he turned for reassurance from his conductress. Aggie was no longer behind him.

'The whole bet's aff,' came Twister's voice again. 'Ye thought you'd take me fur a mug.'

'Ye are a mug!' A figure behind Twister had appeared under the cover of the fog. 'One fiver, pal-leeze!'

'Ah'm no gie'n him a fiver!'

'Then ye can stay here aw night. You an' that slow bus o' yours.'

'Whit dae ye mean?'

'You shouldna' be so careless as tae leave the ignition key in yer bus.'

'You give me that key, hen, or I'll … '

'Ye'll whit? A fiver richt noo or we drive aff wi' the key.'

Suddenly Twister was lying on the ground holding his head. He had never been punched so hard in his life. He thought about trying to stand up, then thought again. His hand found the wallet inside his jacket. He pulled out ten 10-shilling notes.

Aggie snatched them from him and threw the ignition key down.

'But how could ye drive that tram so fast in this fog and know when tae stoap?' he enquired meekly.

'Easy,' replied Aggie. 'The overhead wire over the mile and a hauf has nine connectors oan their gantries. All ye dae is count them aff when ye hear the current collector hit each gantry. When ye get tae nine ye just stoap. Ye might think yer buses are smart but ye'll no' beat a Glesca tram oan a foggy night. They've goat rails tae follow. A bus is loast in a fog. It's diabolical ye didnae think o' that, Twister, jist diabolical!'

Jimmy's wife was delighted with the two pounds extra he gave her at the end of the week. 'A wee bonus ah goat,' he explained. Big Aggie and old Bob both got a pound and Jimmy held onto one for himself.

And yon Twister? He hasn't been seen in the Renfrew Arms for many a long day.

TRAMLINES

The rush hour over the early evening tram to Maryhill was quiet. Aggie was chatting to an off-duty conductress, Sadie Johnstone.

'So where are ye goin', then?'

'Ah'm meetin' a fella at the shell in the Central Station.'

'Hiv ye been oot wi' him afore?'

'Naw. It's a blind date.'

'Crivens – you've been oan that many blind dates, Sadie, the government should gie ye a free guide dug!'

* * *

'Ah widnae like tae tak a broken pay-packet hame tae you!' remonstrated one wee man to Big Aggie who, as usual, had been 'going her dinger'.

'Ah don't blame ye – ye widnae want a broken pay packet and a broken neck aw on the wan night, wid ye noo?'

* * *

A somewhat harassed woman, surrounded by a bunch of kids got on the Maryhill caur one Saturday afternoon. A regular passenger turned to Aggie and enquired. 'Are they aw her's, Aggie, or is it a picnic?'

'They're hers' alright – an' it's certainly no picnic!'

* * *

The extremely rotund lady sat on the Ruchill tram, her nose in the air, haughtily holding her money, waiting for Aggie to give her a ticket. 'A fourpenny ticket, conductress,' she said in a voice which immediately reminded Aggie of her old headmistress.

'Where did ye get oan fae?' asked Aggie.

The passenger looked Aggie straight in the eye. The tone was authoritative. 'A place, conductress, where we do not end our sentences with prepositions.'

'OK, where did ye get oan fae, fatty?'

* * *

The caur going to Partick Cross was full. Many folks, including some elderly ladies were standing, holding onto the overhead straps as the tram shoogled along.

Big Aggie was taking a fare when one man was foolish enough to observe. 'Hey, you're standin' oan ma feet.'

'Listen, doughheid,' retorted Aggie, 'if you were a gentleman you'd be standin' on yer ain!'

* * *

Big Aggie was called on to give evidence in court following an altercation on her caur.

'Well, ye see, yer lordship. The big fella on the number 22 called the wee wummin a lying nyaff, and the wee wummin hit the big fella on the heid wi' her handbag. Then her pal wi' the wan leg jumped on tap o' the big fella. One thing led to another – and then the fightin' started.'

The auld fella, obviously fleein' drunk, had got on at Charing Cross. He had already given the unwilling company on the lower saloon deck two renditions of, 'I Left my Heart in San Francisco'. When Aggie came for his fare he searched every pocket in vain.

'Looks like ah've left ma money wi' ma heart in San Francisco, darlin',' he smiled at Aggie.

'Well, ah left ma heart back at the depot. Aff, O–F–F, aff!'

*   *   *

The American tourist and his wife were moaning to Aggie about the prices in their Glasgow hotel.

'And another thing. They want to charge us extra for a sea view of your River Clyde,' he drawled.

'Don't pey it,' recommended Aggie. 'Just tell them ye kept yer eyes shut.'

*   *   *

The passenger with the large case got off the number 26 tram under the Hielanman's Umbrella, the railway bridge on Argyle Street below Central Station. As he did so he turned to Big Aggie.

'Well, that's the worst part o' the journey o'er.'

'So where are you going, then?'

'Ah'm emigratin' tae Australia.'

*　　*　　*

Aggie was in one of her more belligerent moods. She commented to a woman customer.

'Isn't that tram inspector that stauns at the corner o' Jamaica Street and Argyle Street a right nyaff.'

'Do you know who I am?' demanded the passenger. 'I'm that nyaff's daughter.'

'Oh. And do you know who I am?' queried Aggie.

'Naw,' came the reply.

'Thank heavens!'

*　　*　　*

The wee drunk on the 18A was soaked to the skin and had the look of the out-of-work upon him. His clothes were worn, his mouth pinched. Slightly built, he had abnormally high shoulders, apparently the result of some spinal deformity, probably the result of rickets. He was a half-penny short in his ticket money.

'Sorry, hen,' he slurred. 'Ah thought ah had enough change. Ah must've had a brainstorm.'

'Listen, sunshine,' observed Aggie, 'the nearest you ever came to a brainstorm wis a light drizzle in Shawfield.'

'Ah must be gettin' saft,' she muttered, as she slipped him his ticket.

*　　*　　*

One Saturday Aggie was going upstairs when a male passenger cheekily observed. 'Hey, Aggie. Ah see ye've goat oan red bloomers the day. Here's me wi' a yellow scarf, an' a Partick Thistle fan.'

'Aye,' replied Aggie. 'An' let me tell you, sunshine, yer jist like the Jags. Yer no' scorin' the day!'

*　　*　　*

Wee Inspector Campbell was on board the tram. For once he thought he would be civil and declare a truce with Aggie.

'The depot band played Beethoven last night, Mrs MacDonald.'

'Oh, aye. Who wan?'

*   *   *

A regular woman passenger got over-familiar with Aggie. 'Hey, Big Yin. Yer make-up's on a bit thick the day.'

'Listen you. You'd need tae get yours burned aff wi' a welder's torch doon at John Brown's.'

*   *   *

The sweet-faced, rather quaint old lady, sat with her ticket money in her hand as Aggie approached. 'A tuppenny ticket, please,' she said.

'Whaur are ye goin', hen?' asked Aggie.

'Oh, that's a very private matter,' replied the old lady.

'Well, hen,' said Aggie patiently. 'Ye see ma ticket machine has to know so ah can ring up the correct fare.'

'Oh, ah understand,' replied the passenger. Putting her lips next to Aggie's ticket machine she whispered. 'Ah'm goin' tae see ma sister.'

*   *   *

Aggie was upstairs collecting fares. Suddenly she recognised a passenger who, the last time he was on her tram, had been drunk and made a nuisance of himself. Her hackles went up and the eyes glinted as she passed over his ticket.

'Ye goat a match, hen?' he demanded.

'Aye. Your face an' ma erse.'

*   *   *

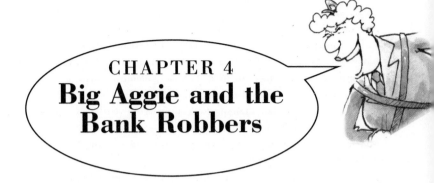

CHAPTER 4
Big Aggie and the Bank Robbers

AGGIE WAS A huge gorgon of indeterminate age, five-foot-nine without the benefit of her black boots, and with a chest under which half-a-dozen wee weans could shelter.

Her face was dominated by a massive circle of bright, red lipstick, applied often and inaccurately around her large, ever-moving mouth. The hair was peroxide blonde, tied down with a multitude of kirby grips and overlaid with a conductress's hat, set at a non-regulation angle.

Aggie was shockingly articulate when on full throttle, firing rapid, staccato commands, rich in glottal stops, at decibels reminiscent of a Clyde foghorn.

So, on the well remembered occasion when she met up with some Glasgow hoods, she was able to deal with them in no uncertain manner.

It happened one Thursday morning, as her number 26 tram to Partick shoogled its way over the points west into Argyle Street from London Road. The Standard looked smart, its livery recently repainted and varnished.

Argyle Street was surprisingly quiet for the day before Glasgow's traditional Fair Friday. There were only a few pedestrians about, plus several security vans topping up the cash in branches of banks for the city's eager citizens to spend during their forthcoming holiday.

The July weather overhead was clear and blue, and the pigeons, roosting on the rooftops, chattered excitedly. Glasgow sparkled with promise.

Big Aggie was in fine humour. Tomorrow she would be on her holidays, 'doon the watter', at her sister's in Dunoon. Sails on the River Clyde, pokes of chips, and peace away from that cheekie wee teuchter, Tram Inspector Campbell. She felt exuberant.

The tram stopped at the fare stage at Glassford Street and some passengers boarded. As the tram started off Aggie decided to take a moment to apply some lipstick before collecting fares upstairs. Suddenly she was rudely bumped from behind. Aggie's bosom heaved indignantly and she turned to remonstrate with the person responsible. Immediately her arms were grabbed by two figures wearing cloth bonnets and scarves over their faces, who forced her inside the lower saloon deck.

'Jist you keep yer mooth closed and you'll no' get hurtit,' was the muffled instruction from one of the thugs. Aggie gasped as she saw the pickaxe handle and sneering eyes. One was tall and thin, his partner small, tubby, sweating and breathing heavily.

The few passengers on the lower deck looked around, aghast.

'Hey, this is a number 26 to Partick, boys,' stated Aggie, starting to get to grips with the situation. 'No' a stagecoach.'

'Listen you, an' listen good,' came the reply. 'We've just taken a few bob oot the Bank o' Scotland at Ingram Street. Just tae help some poor folk in Glesca – us!' He laughed. 'The polis'll no' be lookin' for us on an auld tram.'

'A'll hiv ye know this tram might be auld but it has just been re-decorated. New seat covers up on top too. It's in fine condition,' came Aggie's indignant reply.

'OK, yer tram's just great, hen. Noo, shut it and listen tae me. Nae mair passengers are tae cum oan board – and naebuddy gets aff – they'd tell the polis, see? Noo, you an' me, hen, we'll just go an' see yer driver an' tell him no' tae be stoapin'. Ma pal here will watch fae the platform tae make sure that naebuddy gets oan or aff.'

Aggie, with the handle-wielding thug directly behind, staggered her way up the aisle. At the front platform, driver Jimmy stood staring ahead as the tram advanced over the Jamaica Street points. Aggie shouted through to him. 'Hey, Jimmy! We've been hijacked. Ye've no' tae stoap until this comedian behind me tells ye.' Then added, 'It must be Open Day at Barlinnie.'

Jimmy swung his head round and saw the robber behind Aggie.

'Ye heard her. Keep goin' til ah tell ye tae stoap.' And then addressing Aggie, the gruff voice snarled, 'An' you, shut yer noise! Cut the funnies. Right back tae the front platform, an' act normal, hen. Noo remember. Naebuddy aff or oan!'

The tram, perhaps reflecting Jimmy's nervousness, pulled away with a couple of unsure jolts, jiggling its worried contents over a series of bends, before picking up pace with a continual clunking and determined whine from the bogie.

But hardly had Aggie and the robber returned to the rear platform when a passenger, gaily whistling, came down the stairs. His face changed to an expression of disbelief as Aggie said, 'We've been hijacked by Laurel and Hardy here. You'll need tae go back up top.'

'Listen, you,' came the voice from behind the conductress. 'Jist you dae as yer telt or you'll naw see yer man the nicht.'

'Is that a threat or a promise, son?' rasped Aggie. 'Ah've goat tae tell ye ah'm no' impressed wi' you two. Anybuddy wi' hauf a brain wid hae hijacked a taxi. It's diabolical ye've taken ower a tram. That's whit it is, diabolical! The good Lord must love scruff, because he certainly made plenty o' youse!'

'Nae mere wisecracks fae you! Hey, whit's the caur stoppin' fur? Yer driver wis told no' tae stoap.'

The tram had indeed stopped and a small, uniformed official, with bristling moustache and manner to match, stepped onto the platform.

'Now, Mrs MacDonald,' came the familiar, smug voice of Corporation Tram Inspector Campbell. 'What have I told you time and time again about letting passengers ride on the platform? There appears to be plenty of seats inside.'

'Aye, well you tell them yersel' tae sit doon, Inspector,' came the reply from Aggie. The tone of her voice should have given him a hint that all was not normal, but he turned to the two men, 'Now, gentlemen … ' Then his face turned white and he looked at Aggie for confirmation of the nightmare.

'Whit's keepin' ye then, Inspector Campbell,' smiled Aggie, 'you're the wee man that knows a' the regulations. You're no' gonnae shilly-shally, ah hope.'

'You! Sit doon inside,' commanded the head villain pointing at Campbell. 'And nae funny business.' The inspector sat meekly inside the lower saloon, his lip trembling, the face ashen.

The bell was rung and off went the number 26 again. However as the tram was nearing the end of Argyle Street, just approaching Kelvingrove Art Gallery, a police car siren was heard behind. Suddenly a black police Rover drew ahead of the tram, slewed across the track and stopped. Jimmy was forced to brake hard, producing a loud angry hiss. The sudden jolt almost threw those standing on the platform off their feet. Three policemen rushed to the rear of the tram – then stopped. A bank robber had his pick handle poised over Aggie's head.

'Stoap, or this big clippie gets it! Anyway, hoo did ye know we wis oan this tram?' He demanded to know.

A police sergeant shouted back, 'Ye were seen waitin' at the fare stage!' Aggie gave her would-be attacker a crippling look of disdain.

Traffic all around came to a halt. Passers-by stared in disbelief at the sight of a Glasgow tram clippie being threatened with a weapon.

'She's oor hostage. We're taking her alang fur oor protection – and we'll hae yer polis car tae,' proclaimed the robber, his handle swinging menacingly at Aggie. But he was then astounded at the sound of his hostage's voice.

'Ah'm no' leavin' ma tram! Ma shift's no' over 'til six!'

'That's all right, Mrs MacDonald,' came a quivering, Highland voice. 'In the circumstances you can go now. It's probably clarified somewhere in section 34 of the regulation book.'

Aggie's response was immediate.

'Ah'm nut goin' nowhere!' Aggie drew herself up to her full height, and straightened her back, thereby causing an immediate increase to her significant frontage. The cheeks were scarlet, the eyes ice. She looked the thug straight in the eyes. 'Noo, sunshine, whit are ye goany dae?'

The situation was clear. Big Aggie had become hostile.

The would-be gangster looked at the three large policemen standing ready with truncheons drawn, and then again at Aggie. A shiver ran through him. His voice was somewhat subdued as he addressed his partner in crime.

'Whit'll we dae noo, Wullie. Should we mak a run for it?'

Aggie's voice came again before Wullie could reply. 'Naebuddy gets aff this tram until they've paid their fare. That's fourpence each.'

'You've goat tae be kiddin', missis.'

'Ah ... never ... kid.' The words were slow, deliberate.

The robbers were left in no doubt. The thug with the pick handle dropped it to his side while he fumbled for change in a trouser pocket. That was his mistake. Aggie had the weapon out of his grasp in one movement. A quick lunge and a swish of air preceded the blurred swing of the heavy handle as it cracked his head. Before anyone could move the other thug suffered a similar fate. It was only the intervention of the Glasgow constabulary which prevented serious injury.

As he was being handcuffed the small, fat thug looked up at Aggie through dazed eyes. 'Did ye gie me ma ticket, hen?'

'Aye, an' any time ye want it punched just come oan ma tram.'

A *Glasgow Evening Times* photographer who had hurried to the scene got an excellent view of the stramash. In the next edition a large photograph appeared under the heading:

Bank Robbers Thwarted by Glasgow Tram Clippie

Readers of the newspaper who were regular travellers on the trams immediately knew it would be Big Aggie. Many of them felt a degree of sympathy for the two villains.

The printed quote from Aggie was predictable. 'They might steal oot the Bank o' Scotland but they were nut takin' a free hurl oan ma tram. They're just genuine scruff – wid sook the paper efter a fish supper they would. Imagine hijackin' a tram. Diabolical, that's whit it is. Diabolical!'

Aggie enjoyed the photograph. It made her look slimmer and younger. She took a copy to show her sister in Dunoon.

And as for Inspector Campbell – well his shaking hands couldn't find the incident covered in section 34. That was bad enough but worse was to follow. He was told by the General Manager to give Aggie a commendation certificate, and a reward when she returned after the Fair!

Sometimes Inspector Campbell secretly wondered if God really was a member of the Wee Free.

TRAMLINES

Aggie was on the platform of a Riddrie tram, shouting at a passing policeman. 'Officer. Quick! Ma driver's in a fight wi' a passenger.'

The officer jumped on the platform and asked. 'How long's it been going on then, conductress?'

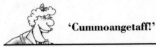
'Aboot twinty minutes.'

'An' you're only *now* asking the law to get involved?'

'Well, up tae noo ma driver wis winnin'!'

*   *   *

Aggie's stationary tram was suddenly jolted. A car had run into its rear.

Aggie alighted and found the white-faced car driver, busy inspecting the damage to his vehicle.

Aggie slowly looked him up and down, and then demanded. 'Tell me, hoo dae ye stoap when we're no' here?'

*   *   *

Aggie's driver, Jimmy Tamson, had been stopped by the Glasgow police for reckless driving. They had given him a ticket.

'What am ah supposed to do wi' this?' he bemoaned to Aggie.

'Keep it, Jimmy. If you manage to collect three o' them, ye probably get a wee prize.'

*   *   *

The tram to Shieldhall was going at a snail's pace. Wee Inspector Campbell was checking tickets halfway up the lower saloon, and taking his time about it! Aggie stood on the rear platform watching him.

Looking back towards her the inspector shouted, 'Is this lad under sixteen?'

'Well, he wis when he goat oan!'

*   *   *

Some passengers on the old open-fronted trams put their luggage on the front platform, in beside the driver. A wee man placed his large metal

box beside Jimmy, then raced round to board in the normal manner, only to be told by Aggie that the tram was full and he couldn't get on.

'But ah'm the man wi' the tin chest,' he pleaded.

'Ah don't care if you've goat a wally erse, yer no' gettin' oan.'

Aggie's tram stopped at a fare stage on Sauchiehall Street one Friday night. There stood an unsteady, red-faced man holding a fish supper.

'Don't you worry, hen,' he slurred. 'Ah'm no' goan oan yer tram drunk wi' chips.'

'Listen, pal,' replied Aggie, 'ye didnae get drunk wi' chips!'

* * *

Aggie was always being confided in by her passengers. One well-heeled lady told Aggie that she intended leaving money to her family. 'In that way,' she said, 'they'll still remember me efter a couple o' years.'

'Well, ah'm goin' tae leave ma lot a pile o' debts,' replied Aggie. 'That way they'll still be talkin' aboot me twenty years efter ah've gone!'

* * *

'Aggie. Dae ye think there is any woman oan this earth who really knows where her husband is every night?' asked one anxious lady passenger, just recently married.

'Aye. Ye call them widows!'

* * *

A passenger, alighting at Glasgow Cross, commented to Aggie that it had been the smoothest journey he had ever had on a Glasgow tram.

'Ah'm no surprised,' commented Aggie. 'Ma temporary driver only found out how the brakes worked at Bridgeton Cross.'

* * *

A young woman on the lower deck had twins of 18 months, both boys. All the other ladies onboard were admiring them. One of the regulars turned to Aggie. 'They're exactly alike. Isn't she lucky.'

'Yer dead right – they're her big sister's.'

*　*　*

'If you ever left the trams, what do you think Inpector Campbell would do?' asked Jimmy the driver.

'Him! He'd need an operation.'

'Whit fur?'

'Tae get the smile aff his face!'

*　*　*

Aggie had taken the opportunity, during a quiet time, to repair her make-up. As the tram trundled along, out came the perfume bottle. She applied it generously.

At the next stop, which was Anniesland, wee Inspector Campbell came onboard. He sniffed a number of times before commenting. 'This tram smells like a brothel, Mrs MacDonald.'

'Speakin' fae experience, then?' replied Aggie.

*　*　*

44

The tram to Bridgeton Cross was full, passengers crushed together, bodies hanging onto straps and anything else available. A wee man was sandwiched between two matronly ladies.

'Dae ye want a tuppeny one?' asked Aggie. 'Or should ah go and find a meenister tae make it legal?'

✳   ✳   ✳

'Aggie,' opined Jimmy her driver one day, 'sure that Tram Inspector Campbell's goat funny wee eyes like a hen?'

'Yer right, Jimmy,' agreed Aggie. 'He's cock-eyed. Wan eye's goin' fur a message an' the ither's comin' back wi' the change.'

✳   ✳   ✳

CHAPTER 5
Big Aggie and the Wedding

ALTHOUGH A BIT of a tyrant on board her tram, Aggie, at heart, was really a romantic. As Jimmy Tamson used to say, 'Ye can always tell when Aggie fancies a fella. The eyelids go all of a flutter. Like seagulls roon a sludge boat.'

Aggie's predilection for the opposite sex was also one of the reasons for her ever fluctuating hemline. When shorter skirts were in vogue it was noticeable that the Glasgow male became chivalrous when climbing the stairs to the upper deck. Indeed, going 'up top' one day was just what Aggie was doing when she first heard of the wedding.

As she was mounting the top stairs she heard a woman's voice exclaim, 'Here's Big Aggie noo. Ah'll ask if she could help.'

To which Aggie immediately rasped, 'Here's ma heid, ma erse is jist comin'.'

Two ladies sat with expectant faces on the Glaswegian's favourite place on a tram – the front seat directly above the driver's platform. 'Aggie,' began Ginty MacDonald, a regular daily customer and Aggie's second cousin – twice removed. (Twice removed as Aggie reckoned Ginty had done at least two moonlight fittings on rent days!) 'Ye'll remember ah told ye ma daughter Sadie's gettin' merrit soon. Well, ah wis jist talkin' over the arrangements with ma frien' here.' She indicated the nodding lady beside her, resplendent in transparent plastic mac, curlers and rain-mate. 'Well, the problem is, Aggie, we're stuck fur transport tae take the guests frae the church tae the reception, and ... as the number of guests is jist aboot fifty ... ' She looked sideways at her friend for encouragement, '... and the church and Co-operative hall are both on your route ... well, the question is, wid it be possible tae hire yer tram?'

Aggie straightened up, her face pensive. 'That's a new yin oan me,' she thought. 'A've heard o' trams being hired tae take weans oot

47

tae the country, and specials fur fitba and things, but never fur a weddin'.'

If she asked that Tram Inspector Campbell she knew what kind of an answer he would give. Mind you, a tram car would be quite romantic, quite different, quite like marriage ... traditional an' that, she mused.

Ginty's voice came again. 'And of course, Aggie, we wid be delighted to have you at the weddin' tae.'

Aggie's heart quickened. She hadn't been to a wedding in years. 'When's the date o' the weddin'?' she asked anxiously.

'It's oan Saturday, the ninth o' August, at three o'clock, Aggie.'

'Aw naw! Ah'm workin' that day.' However as someone who did not give up easily, Aggie added quickly, 'But ah might manage the reception. Noo, let me think aboot the hiring o' a caur.'

Aggie could hardly wait until the tram reached the terminus at Duntocher. She needed some advice from Jimmy. He might know. Efter a', she reasoned, he'd been on the trams fur dunkeys.

The tram had just wheezed to a stop when she stuck her head through into the driving platform. 'Jimmy. Here's a right stoater o' a question fur ye. Can ye hire a tram? You know, fur a private function.'

'Aye, if ye're the Lord Provost or somebuddy like that,' Jimmy replied flippantly.

'It's fur a weddin', Jimmy.' said Aggie, disappointed at Jimmy's initial reaction.

'A weddin'! Can they no' afford a taxi?'

'Naw, naw, it's fur the guests. Transportin' them frae the church tae the Co-operative hall fur the reception. They're baith oan oor route alang Dumbarton Road. Jings, we could maybe dae it oorselves.' Aggie's eyes gleamed as her imagination raced. 'Listen, Jimmy. We could stick a notice oan the front sayin' 'private', and no' let oanybuddy else oan, pick up the guests at the church and just let them aff at the Co-op. It's only aboot three stops. Dead easy, eh?'

'Holy Toledo, Aggie! Ye'd get us wur books!'

But Aggie was carried away. It would be a wonderful day. 'An' ah could get Wee Bella tae finish ma shift, and ah'd join everybody in the Co-op fur the purvey, an' that.'

'Noo ah understaun', Aggie,' replied Jimmy. 'You've been invited! Ah might have known. Tell ye whit, ah'll have a wee think aboot this. But it's no' something ah wid want tae rush intae, mind ye.'

During the following week it was noticeable that Aggie was acting differently. Passengers who would hitherto have been given short shrift were treated surprisingly well, even courteously. Aggie was in another world. Her face was radiant and she hummed as she went about her work. Anybody listening closely would have recognised Mendelssohn's 'Wedding March'.

But Jimmy remained doubtful. It was a bit of a risk. What if they were reported and Tram Inspector Campbell got to hear about it?

Jimmy finally agreed to do it, but only on condition that they didn't put up any 'private' notices and that ostensibly, at any rate, it was just a normal tram service.

When next the mother of the bride was onboard, Aggie made a beeline for her. 'A've fixed it, ' she confided. 'Mind you, it'll cost ye aboot nine shillings in total fur tickets.'

'Great, Aggie. Wait 'til a tell everybody a've hired a tram.'

Aggie's face fell. 'Well, ye see, Ginty, it's a sort of … well … a private arrangement ah've made. Ye cannae tell onybuddy in advance. Anyway, it'll be a great surprise when yer guests aw come oot o' the church and there's oor caur waitin' fur them. Okay? And another thing. Ye'll need tae hae a word wi' yer meenister. Ah reckon he'll need tae finish dead on half-past three, then you get the photos taken heap pronto, fur ma tram will be ootside at exactly a quarter tae four. We canny hing about ye ken. We'd haud up the hale transport system.'

'Nae problem, Aggie. Yer a right pal. I'll fix up tae see the meenister and tell him tae keep an eye oan his watch. He can be awfa long winded at times. Furthermore ah'll make sure ma daughter turns up at the church on time. Nane o' this business o' being five minutes late.'

'That's smashin',' replied Aggie. But her mind was elsewhere – thinking of a new hat for the big day.

Jimmy was duly informed of the arrangement and grudgingly agreed.

✳   ✳   ✳

The Saturday of the wedding arrived. The forecast said it would be high pressure, warm, a real lovely day. Aggie was up at the crack of dawn. 'My it must be wonderful to be a new bride,' she thought.

Big Aggie and Jimmy reported to the Partick Depot at 12

o'clock to start their shift. Aggie looked extra smart, having taken hours to put on her make-up. She had a battered old suitcase in her hand which was quickly dispatched into the cubby-hole under the stairs of the tram. 'If anybuddy touches that, ah'll swing fur them,' she informed Jimmy. 'It's goat ma outfit and the new hat.'

The tram duly shoogled its way out the depot and along Dumbarton Road. At exactly three o'clock they reached the terminus at Duntocher. The overhead and the seats were quickly turned around. Amazingly no passengers were waiting to take the tram, and the caur set off empty back into town.

The tram had to pass four fare stops before they got to the church and Aggie was determined not to pick up passengers if she could possibly avoid it. After all, she rationalized, there would be a number 9 and a 26 coming behind them in a couple of minutes time.

At the first stop the fare stage was empty and they simply flew past. However at the next stage a wee man in a cloth bunnet, somewhat unsteady on his feet, left the pavement and made his way out to the rails to meet the oncoming tram. Aggie's heart sank. She knew him. Wee Hughie, a daily regular whom she had yet to see sober. As the tram slowed he grabbed the rail and was seated in the lower saloon before Aggie had time to say anything. As she took his fare he looked up, his face red and agitated. 'Wis ah oan yer tram yesterday, Aggie?'

'Ye certainly were,' replied Aggie. A glint in her eye.

'And did ah hae a cairry-oot wi' me?'

'Ye certainly did.'

'Thank Goad. Ah thought ah hud lost aw ma money! An' look. A've goat another wee wan the day,' he slurred, holding up a half bottle of whisky.

'Aye, well you behave yersel'. This tram's jist aboot tae be full o' some important folks.'

'Oh, is that so? An' am ah no' important, Aggie?'

'Aye, you're very important,' replied the conductress, opting to humour him under the circumstances.

No more passengers joined, and soon the tram was thankfully within sight of the church. Aggie was much relieved to see the pavement full of smart looking folks all in their Sunday best. At the front of this crowd was Ginty MacDonald, waving when she saw Aggie's head peering out from the caur's rear platform.

As the tram stopped, the wedding guests clambered onboard,

leaving the inside seats in the lower saloon free for the young bride and groom. Last on were the newlyweds who sat down to much clapping and cheering from their guests.

'Aw yer looking real lovely, hen,' exclaimed Aggie to the young bride. And then turning to her new husband asked, 'Ur ye no' throwin' oot 'lucky pennies', son?'

The groom's face fell. 'Ah forgot the money. Ah left it oan the mantelpiece.'

'Dinna worry,' replied Aggie, 'here's a pile o' ha'pennies.' And so saying she gave him a handful of coins from her cash bag. 'This wedding's costin' me a packet', she thought.

At the fare stage a group of wee boys had miraculously materialised. 'Hard up! Hard up! Where's the scrammy?' they shouted.

As the tram moved off, the young groom moved to the platform and threw the coins high and wide towards the pavement. They seemed to hang in the air for a moment, before the noisy pack of urchins was on them.

They had now three further fare stops to pass en route to the Co-operative hall. The tram was virtually full, only a couple of seats remaining unoccupied upstairs.

Aggie stood on the platform as the next stop approached. A couple of people were waiting and they came forward from the pavement in anticipation of boarding the tram. Aggie's arm went straight out and she bellowed, 'Wur full. There'll be anither caur alang in a wee minute!'

However at the second stop, just before Balshagray Avenue, Aggie saw her worst nightmare – the small figure of Tram Inspector Campbell leaving the fare stage, his hand outstretched. 'Aw naw, no' him! It's no' fair, that's whit it is, in fact it's jist diabolical,' she muttered to herself. Jimmy had no option but to stop.

As Inspector Campbell came onto the platform he immediately surmised that the passengers were extremely well dressed for a Saturday afternoon in Glasgow. His amazed gaze took in the bride, wearing her white lace dress, gored with georgette, and the veil with its cluster of bride's blossom at the ears. Beside her sat the proud groom, flushed and expectant.

Campbell's eyes narrowed and he gave Aggie a knowing look before shouting out, 'Have your tickets ready for inspection, please.'

The bride's mother, Ginty MacDonald, sitting on a seat just beyond the young pair, yelled back. 'Ave goat a' the tickets here, Inspector. Forty-eight o' them tae be exact.'

The Inspector moved along the passageway and spent time closely examining the roll of offered tickets. He then made his way back to the rear platform where Aggie stood. Campbell put on his most officious face.

'Ah'm no' daft, Mrs MacDonald,' he observed in a solemn voice. 'Ah can see whit's happening here. The misuse of public transport, that's whit it is. Not allowing the general Glasgow public onto a tram is extremely serious.' His eyes gleamed. He finally had a major offence with which he could report Aggie. It was the day he had dreamed about. He was just about to get Aggie fired!

An annoying voice rang out, disturbing his fantasy. 'Hey you, wee yin! Ye didnae inpect ma ticket.' Campbell turned to see the indignant Hughie lurching down the passageway towards him, ticket held high in the air.

'Are you a guest with this wedding party?' growled the inspector, upset at both the reference to his size, and the possibility that there could be a real passenger on Aggie's tram.

'Whit weddin'? Ah don't know nuthin' aboot a weddin'.' Then Hughie noticed the blushing bride. 'Aw, hen, are ye just merrit. Aw the best. Huv a wee drink.' And he produced from his jacket pocket the half-bottle. He held it up, inspected its contents, and then slurred. 'Sorry, hen, itsh all done.'

Inspector Campbell took Hughie's ticket, examined it carefully, before giving it back. A look of defeat slowly crossed his bureaucratic face.

'You sail awfa close to the wind, Mrs MacDonald. Jist remember. Ah'm watchin' you – very carefully.' As the tram halted at the juction of Crow Road he hopped off, looking back wistfully at the departing vehicle.

'Ah'm awfa sorry if ah got ye into oany trouble, Aggie.' said Ginty.

'Nut a problem at all,' Aggie reassured her. 'Noo, where is that wee Hughie? Come here you!' As she planted a big kiss on Hughie's lips a cheer went up from the wedding guests seated in the lower saloon.

'Hey, is this ma lucky day?' exclaimed Hughie. 'Ah always said ye wur wan in a million, Aggie.'

'Aye, an' so's yer chances,' replied Aggie, now back to her usual self.

The reception in the Co-operativeHhall proved a great success. Aggie, with her new wide-brimmed black and red pan velvet hat, thoroughly enjoyed herself, and took part in almost every dance.

The surprise guest of honour was wee Hughie, who quietly sat in a happy stupor in a corner, drinking a continual stream of 'wee goldies' bought, of course, by a grateful Big Aggie MacDonald.

TRAMLINES

The woman passenger on the Blairdardie tram had exchanged words with Aggie in the past and both were eyeing each other up. The passenger could not resist a comment. 'See you. You've enough paste oan yer face as wid make a pile o' pancakes!'

'Aye, an' you've enough fat oan yir erse tae fry them in!'

* * *

Big Aggie was in good form, quietly singing the latest hit from the Top 20 as she took fares on a 29 bound for Maryhill. It was, 'She wears Red Feathers and a Hulu-Hulu Skirt', normally sung by by Guy Mitchell.

'Hey, Aggie, ah fancy you in red feathers and a hulu-hulu skirt,' observed one man, a daily regular.

'Well, forget it, sunshine. Ah'm certainly no' ticklin' your fancy!'

* * *

'Hey, Aggie! This caur tae Mount Florida is overcrowded,' moaned one large lady as she swung from side to side with the motion of the tram.

'Away an bile yer heid!' retorted Aggie. 'Ye've goat a strap aw tae yersel', huvin't ye?'

*   *   *

Aggie was not in a good mood. She stormed up and down the tram, shouting instructions to all and sundry.

'Hey, Aggie!' replied one of the recipients of her tongue. 'Ah' think you just became a clippie so you could tell people where to get aff.'

'Aye, yer right. An' this is your stop. Cummoangetaff!'

*   *   *

'Excuse me, miss,' ventured one rather timid passenger to Aggie. 'Does this tram stop at Clydeside?'

'Well if it doesnae, there's goin' tae be one helluva splash!'

*   *   *

It was late afternoon and the number 9 to Dalmuir West caur was full to overflowing. It had been a filthy, wet day and the floor was slippy, the windows all steamed up. Aggie was up to 'high doh' trying to collect fares while limiting those getting on at each stop. It was pandemonium and she was harassed.

Two neatly dressed young men with polite American accents, standing on the lower deck, having given up their seats to two ladies, accosted Aggie as she tried to squeeze past.

'Miss, we'd like to tell you how to obtain eternal life,' said one with a charming smile.

'Thanks, son,' replied Aggie,' but ah don't think ah could stand it.'

*   *   *

One of the passengers was an ex-conductress, wee Bella, who had left the trams some months previously when she married.

'So how's it goin' wi' you an that new man o' yours?' enquired Aggie.

'See him,' replied Bella, 'ah've goat him eatin' oot ma haun.'

'Ach, well,' replied Aggie, 'saves ye hivin' tae wash the dishes.'

'eatin' oot ma haun'

*   *   *

An old lady, who was taking her time in getting off a tram at George Square called out to Aggie. 'Wait a wee minute, hen. Don't ring yer bell. Ah'm gettin' on you know.'

Aggie replied. 'In that case you'd better sit doon. Ah could've sworn you were gettin' aff.'

*   *   *

The tram was full and only one person got off at the stop on Argyle Street.

'Wan inside only!' shouted Aggie.

The impatient crowd surged forward but were halted by the thundering voice of Aggie.

'Ah said wan, no' fifty-wan!'

*   *   *

The well dressed lady did not even bother to look as she asked Aggie. 'Does this tram go Purr-tick, conductress?'

'Naw, hen,' replied Aggie. 'It goes squeak, squeak alang the rails.'

*   *   *

It was the Sabbath and Aggie was just leaving the Govan Depot after finishing her shift. She met two young girls, regular customers on her route, who took her tram to school each day. The girls were today dressed up to the 'nines', with high heels, lipstick and make-up.

As she passed them on the pavement, the girls smiled at Aggie, who spoke out of the corner of her mouth.

'Ur youse just sixteen oan a Sunday?'

*   *   *

The tram had stopped. Before boarding two students shouted in to Aggie, standing on the rear platform.

'Does this tram go to the Yoonie?'

'Naw. There's enough goes aff the rails up there.'

*   *   *

The rather rotund lady had on her best stole, fur coat and kid gloves. The tram was almost empty and she was clearly keen to converse.

'You know, miss,' she confided in Aggie. 'I've been on planes and ships, not just trams. Travel broadens one, you know.'

'Been roon the world a few times, then?' remarked Aggie.

*   *   *

The young couple on the number 3A white caur were having a dispute as Aggie approached.

'Ah'm urny no' goin''

'Ye ur sot.'

'No ah'm no'!'

'Ferrs, pal-leeze,' asked Aggie, and the pair displayed student passes. The quizzical look on her face brought a response from the young man.

'Wur goin' tae the Yoonie.'

'Oh, aye. Studying foreign languages, then?'

It was a December Saturday night, and a somewhat fu' wee man boarded Aggie's Scotstoun-bound tram and immediately gave the assembled passengers a rendition of, 'I'm Dreaming of a White Christmas.' Aggie's eyes were glinting. She waited for him to produce his fare. Eventually he produced a penny. 'Hoo far will ye let me go fur a penny, pet? Gees a wee cheeper.'

'Listen, Bing,' she commented. 'Ah widnae let ye kiss ma erse for a fiver. Aff. O–F–F, aff!'

Aggie was having an altercation with a passenger who was disputing his fare. He was clearly unhappy with Aggie.

'See you. Ye gie me the dry boke.'

The massive bosom heaved. 'An' see you. Ye gie me the right fare or yer aff this tram.'

The wee man gettin' off the tram on Argyle Street had obviously had rickets. A couple of passing boys shouted at him, 'Hey you. Yer bowly!'

Aggie stuck her head out the tram and bawled at them.

'Leave that wee man alane or he'll get his horse tae run ye doon!'

CHAPTER 6
Big Aggie has an Admirer

IN THE TRAM depot one day Jimmy couldn't help but notice that Aggie's wedding ring was now on her index finger. 'Aggie, ye've goat yer wedding ring oan the wrang finger.'

'Aye, ah merrit the wrang man.'

'Huv you two been having a fight again?'

'Ye could say that. He's a lazy lump. Been oan the buroo so lang they'll be invitin' him tae go oan the staff outin' tae Blackpool! But ah don't really want tae talk too much aboot it.'

It was well known that Aggie and her man, whom few people had ever seen, went through periods of, shall we say, difficulty. It was during this one that Aggie acquired her admirer.

It all started when, in an early morning rush-hour, the number 32 was shoogling along with a full complement of passengers. Aggie had just come down from the upper deck where she had been giving a boy laldie for being cheeky. She rasped out, 'Ferrs, p-lease,' and busied herself collecting them in on the lower saloon.

The lower deck had 10 people holding precariously onto straps, their balance continually challenged by the motion of the tram. A tall gentlemen in a blue suit rose to give his seat to the lady standing swaying beside him. As Aggie approached him for his fare he turned and looked at her. Aggie's heart missed a beat. He was a dead ringer for Tony Curtis, her very favourite movie star! 'Oh, heavens,' she thought, 'ah only took a wee minute to apply ma make-up at the terminus.' She smiled at him and he smiled back, a gleaming gold tooth showing in an otherwise perfect set. The eyes flashed and he held out his fourpence for his ticket. For a moment Aggie couldn't speak. She was overcome. She stuck his ticket in his fingers and moved on.

It was immediately noticeable to Aggie's passengers that something had happened. The next time she spoke, the tone was softer, the words different from her usual repertoire. 'Please have your fare money ready, ladies and gentlemen.' A number of the regular passengers looked up to see who the new conductress was, and were astounded to see it was still Aggie. 'The corporation must have been givin' them elocution lessons,' opined one passenger.

At the terminus at Provanmill, Jimmy could not help but notice that Aggie was preening herself somewhat more than usual. For once the lipstick was applied with care and the eyebrows swept back with a wet finger. 'Jings you're applying the make-up thick an' fast. Made up wi' yer auld man then?'

'Naw! That yin will be gettin' sent back tae his mammy soon! If ye must know, well, ah saw this fulla oan the caur this morning. Handsome, isnae the word fur it. He'd put a smile on oany wumman's face.'

'But did he fancy you, Aggie, that's the question?' asked Jimmy.

'Oh, aye, ah could tell he did.'

'So, whit did he say tae ye?'

'Well, nothin' really. But us wummin always know these things.'

Jimmy turned his head away, a smile on his face.

'So dae ye think ye'll see him again?'

'Och aye. He's dead keen. Be oan oor caur the morn' fur sure.'

And Aggie was right. She saw "Tony" getting on at Castle Street the following morning. The tram wasn't so full and he managed to get an aisle seat in the lower saloon. Aggie dashed up the stairs and sat down for a minute looking in her compact mirror. Then she walked slowly down the stairs, chest full out, and with a slight wiggle of her hips. 'Please have your money ready, ladies and gentlemen.' The voice was straight from a 'B' movie.

"Tony" looked round and smiled. 'See,' she thought, 'ah'm right. He does fancy me rotten!'

'A fourpenny ticket, conductress,' he said, his eyes sweeping the fulsome figure.

'Where are you going to, sir,' asked Aggie, the eyelashes all a flutter.

'To the Coo-caddens, miss,' he replied, his eyes dropping to observe that no ring adorned the wedding finger. 'My, my,' he continued, 'ah see you're a treasure waiting to be found.'

Aggie blushed. Afterwards she reckoned it was the first time she had done that since wee Peter Fletcher had kissed her at the school gate – and that was after her first morning at primary school!

'Oh, you right Romeo, you,' she replied, giving him a nudge on the arm before moving onto the next row of passengers. When she came back down the aisle towards him he gave Aggie a big wink.

'Oh heavens, Jimmy,' she again confided to Jimmy at the terminus, 'That yin fair fancies me. Ah'm aw o' a dither.'

'Yer right aboot that, Aggie. Ye huvnae turned roon the seats an' we leave in two minutes.'

'Neither ah huv. Ma heid's fair birlin'!'

'Who is this "Tony Curtis" oanyway,' asked Jimmy amid the clatter of seats being knocked forward.

'Ah don't know, Jimmy. He speaks awfa nice but ah canny quite place the accent.'

'You watch yersel' an' no' dae oanything silly,' continued Jimmy. 'Remember Aggie, nothing beats peace o' mind. A wee hauf in front o' the fire an' the MacFlannels oan a Saturday night oan the wireless. That's whit ah say. Gae me that an' ah widnae ca' the King my cousin!'

'Yer right, Jimmy. But don't you worry. Ah'll no' dae oanything silly.'

But she couldn't get "Tony" out of her mind. Every day she lingered a little more when taking his ticket money, and every day she seemed to Jimmy even more besotted. That is until the Friday morning "Tony" asked her out.

She had just given him his ticket when he ventured. 'I was wondering, miss, as ah'm a bit of a stranger to your lovely city, if you would do me the honour of perhaps tripping the light fantastic with me … say at the Denny Pally tomorrow night?'

'Oooo.' Words stuck in Aggie's mouth. She had dreamed of this moment. At last a knight in shining armour had come to rescue her.

She found her voice. 'Ah'd love to,' she smiled, nervous as a kitten. 'But ye see, ah work Saturday nights. Ah cannae get aff.'

It was then that he opted to play his ace card. Show her that he knew people in authority.

'Don't worry, miss. My uncle is a high-heid-yin, as you would say, with the Glasgow Transport authorities. You see his sister, that is my mother, moved to Hampshire, where I was born, but I've kept in touch with Uncle Colin over the years. I'll have a wee word with him and I'm sure he'll get your shift changed.'

The expression on Aggie's face slightly changed, the voice deepened. 'Whit's yer uncle's name?'

'You'll maybe know him. He's an Inspector, a Colin Campbell.'

"Tony" watched horrified as thunder rolled over Aggie's brow and lightening flashed in her eyes. 'A bloody Campbell, and an English wan at that! Ah might have known. Wauchlin' yer way intae ma good books. Well, ah'm Aggie MacDonald, an ye can just massacre somebody else's feet at the jiggin'!'

'But, but … ', he stuttered, his face white with shock.

'Nae buts! When ah want yer opinion ah'll ask fur it, ya big chanty wrasler ye!'

"Tony" was off at the next stop before the tram had hissed to a halt.

As Aggie collected fares the following afternoon one schoolboy got cheeky with her. She rang the bell for the tram to stop, held onto his ear and threw him off the tram. A regular passenger observed. 'Glad tae see yer back tae yersel', Aggie.'

TRAMLINES

It was early Saturday night and the smartly dressed, young man standing in the queue on Hope Street shouted into the tram platform where Aggie was standing.

'Does this tram go tae the dancin'?'

'Naw, son. It wid make a terrible mess o' yer shoes.'

✳   ✳   ✳

'Hey you,' exclaimed the irate, red-faced, male passenger addressing Aggie. 'Is there any danger o' this caur gettin' tae the Kelvin Hall in time for the first hoose o' the circus?'

'Listen,' countered Aggie, 'oany mair cheek and they'll be wan clown short the night.'

❋   ❋   ❋

The passenger with the grandfather clock was frustrated because, as the front platform was already full with boxes, he had to take the clock inside the lower saloon. As luck would have it the tram was busy and he had to stand.

Aggie elbowed her way up the aisle collecting fares and managed, with some difficulty, to pass him. Her comment was predictable.

'Can you no' wear a watch like everybuddy else?'

❋   ❋   ❋

It was Aggie's day off and she was going into town. She thought she would try one of the new-fangled trolley buses. As she was about to board the trolley bus a Pakistani conductor barred her way.

'No more room,' he said. 'I'm crammed jam full.'

'Ah don't care whit yer name is, sunshine,' retorted Aggie. 'Ah'm gettin' oan.'

❋   ❋   ❋

The rather large lady with the fur coat spoke to Aggie.

'Conductress, I was really impressed when I got on a tram yesterday. Three men got up to give me their seats.'

'An' did ye take them?'

Aggie was in a good mood and sometimes, when in such a euphoric state, was apt to suddenly burst into song.

One day as her tram stopped in Hope Street the astonished queue heard her in full voice.

'I dream of Jeanie with the light brown hair, wan inside an' two up the stair.'

* * *

There had been a wee accident. The tram to Charing Cross had hit a man whose bike wheels had stuck in the rails. Aggie was duly interviewed by the Glasgow Police.

'Well ye see, officer, the driver started tae stoap but couldnae go slow fast enough tae avoid the back o' the bike.'

* * *

'Well, this is my stop, conductress,' Aggie was informed by the long-winded passenger as the number 29 approached Milngavie. 'It's been a long journey but I'm sure my little stories have kept you going. Do you know, when I came on board your tram I had a headache, but I've now lost it completely.'

'Don't worry, hen, it's no' lost. Ah've goat it!'

* * *

The man sat on the upper deck. He lit up a Woodbine from a paper packet of five and took a long, slow drag, expanding his chest and holding in the smoke, before reluctantly blowing it out between blue lips. Holding the cigarette with his finger and thumb close to the lighted end, he flicked the glowing tip cleanly away with his thumb nail, and slid the now shortened fag carefully back into the flimsy packet. The glowing ember on the tram deck was stubbed out with a heavy boot. Then he suffered a great spasm of coughing.

As Aggie was collecting his fare, he had a particularly loud, racking bout.

'Ah canny understaun' how yer chist is so bad,' commented Aggie. 'Ye only seem tae smoke fags in instalments.'

* * *

One of Aggie's customers had just returned from a weekend in Blackpool. 'Aggie,' she confided. 'The tram fare alang the promenade is twice whit ye'd pey fur the same distance in Glesca'. Scandalous, ain't it?'

'Yer right,' observed Aggie. 'If the English had charged like that at Bannockburn they'd huv won.'

* * *

'Ah saw you an yer man oot shoppin' in Argyle Street on Saturday morning,' observed one regular to Aggie. 'A've got tae tell you, Aggie, ah think he's gettin' gey pigeon chisted.'

'Aye. That's why I love him like ah do.'

The young teenage girl sat on the upper deck sobbing.

'Whit's up, hen?' enquired a sympathetic Aggie.

'Ma boyfriend an' me huv' split up.'

'Listen, hen. Men's just like the Glesca caurs; there'll be anither alang in ten minutes.'

The man standing at the fare stop looked up at Aggie on the platform.

'Hey, you! Whit's the quickest way ah can get tae Glasgow Royal?'

'Easy. Lie doon on they rails in front o' ma tram!'

The queue on Argyle Street had been waiting for the tram for quite a while. They were becoming frustrated.

Two trams, showing the same destination numbers, eventually appeared, travelling slowly, one just a few yards behind the other. When they stopped, a passenger shouted to Big Aggie on the rear platform of the first tram. 'Hey, whit's the big idea? Two trams the gither.'

'Wur winchin'!'

The drunk had got to the belligerent stage. When Aggie asked him for his fare he thought he would be funny. 'Dae ye know, hen. You've goat hair like a lavvy-brush.'

'Is that so, sunshine,' countered Aggie. 'Well let me tell you that yer face is gey clapped-in.'

'Ma face isnae clapped-in.'

'It will be when ma fist removes yer teeth.'

He produced his fare.

CHAPTER 7
Big Aggie
and the Baby

THE OLD STANDARD trams in Glasgow carried many items on their front platforms. Furniture, bags of washing from the steamie, even coffins, empty of course. It was a cheap way to transport small goods around the city.

Aggie's number 9 from Carmyle had made its way up London Road and was stopped at the Fare Stage outside Lewis's departmental store in Argyle Street. Once the departing passengers had disembarked the large queue surged forward. However, as so many of them were heavily laden with purchases, the progress of those going upstairs was painfully slow.

A frustrated voice from the back of the queue of people attempting to board the tram shouted, 'Hey, clippie. Can ye no' gie that lot a shove!'

'Nut oan yer life, pal,' exclaimed Big Aggie, standing on the rear platform watching the hold-up. 'Someboady wance told ma sister tae shove and she ended up wi' twins!'

It took some time before Aggie got everyone aboard and the loaded tram finally was able to move off. Over the next 20 minutes Aggie was kept busy getting around both decks, collecting fares, as the tram happily shoogled along the length of Argyle Street.

However by the time it got to Anniesland Road most of the passengers had disembarked, leaving only a few in the lower saloon. As Aggie rang the bell to start off again, a passenger pointed to a bundle lying on a seat up at the front. 'Aggie, there's a wee wean in a shawl lying here.' Aggie moved along the aisle and looked down on the sleeping, pink face of a small baby.

'Where's its maw?' she asked looking round at the faces. She raised her voice. 'Oanybuddy here loast a wean?' Getting no response she moved to the rear platform and shouted up the stairs. 'Anybuddy

69

lookin' fur a wean up there?'

'Naw thanks, ah've goat eight already,' a voice replied.

'Ah better see Jimmy aboot this', she murmured.

Poking her head round the driver's door she shouted above the rumble of the tram. 'Hey, Jimmy do you know anythin' aboot a wee wean layin' here?'

'Sure ah do, Aggie. It wis in the pram there,' and he indicated a pram sitting beside a couple of boxes on the platform. 'The wee soul wid be gettin' her death o' cauld fae the wind so ah stuck her in the back seat. It's warmer in there.'

'Ya dumplin'! Trust a man. Could ye no' have told me? Where's its maw?'

'Havenae a clue. Is she no' wan o' yer passengers? She must be the person who put the pram oan the caur.'

'Naw, naebuddy knows anythin' aboot the wean.'

Aggie returned to where the baby was now lying with eyes wide open, cooing softly. Aggie gently lifted the bundle and sat on the seat talking to the baby. A couple of the lady passengers joined her, admiring the child.

'Hasn't she goat lovely curly dark hair.'

'And look at those big eyes.'

'Wull break some man's heart wan day.'

'Aye, yer right', commented Aggie. 'But the mither must be breaking her's right noo.' Aggie sighed. 'Ye know ah've always wanted a wean. Ah'm fair enjoying this wee cuddle. The only trouble is the wee soul will be lookin' fur a feed soon, and she'll need her maw fur that.'

'What's going on here, Mrs MacDonald?' A man's voice was heard and Aggie looked up into the officious face of Tram Inspector Campbell. 'You appear to be neglecting your duties and holding passenger's children.'

'Listen, Inspector, this wee soul's loast. She wis in a pram pit ontae the front platform by a passenger.'

'If she's lost, Mrs MacDonald,' came the Highland voice, 'she'll need to go to Lost Property.'

Aggie looked him square in the eye. 'In the name o' the wee man, ur you tellin' me, Inspector, that this wee soul should be pit in a shelf in the Depot?' There were murmurings from the other passengers.

Campbell coughed and cleared his throat. 'Well ... perhaps, Mrs MacDonald, some other, er ... action should be taken.'

'Aye, yer right,' exclaimed Aggie, her face gettin' redder by the minute. 'Tell ye whit, Inspector, YOU haud the wean.' And she thrust the bundle into Campbell's arms.

'But, but ah've never held a child before, Mrs MacDonald,' he moaned.

'Then it'll be a grand experience fur ye. As fur me, ah'm stoappin' this caur and phonin' the polis.'

Aggie stuck her head back through to Jimmy. 'Stoap at the next phone box, Jimmy. Ah'm goin' tae phone the polis aboot this wean.'

When the tram stopped beside a red phone box, the passengers and inspector, still holding the baby, watched as Aggie used the phone. Two minutes later she was back onboard. There was a smile on her face.

'The polis know aw aboot the wean,' she announced. 'The mither's in London Road police station in a terrible state. She apparently put the pram oan oor caur wi' the wean in it, and we moved aff before she could get the wean oot. Poor soul. Anyway a polis car is bringing her here right noo. So we've no' tae move until the polis comes.'

'Whit will I do with the child until then, Mrs MacDonald?' came a quivering male voice.

'Sing tae it, Inspector. But no' in the Gaelic. It'll probably only understaun' English.'

Shortly a police car arrived and the young mother was reunited with her baby and pram. 'Ah wis goin' tae visit ma mither in Partick,' she explained tearfully. 'Ah don't know whit ah wid hae done if onythin' had happened tae ma wee Isabella.'

'Whit a lovely name fur the wee soul,' sympathised Aggie. 'Well you jist stay oan the tram, hen, an' we'll drop ye off at Partick oan oor return journey from Dalmuir.'

'And I must be going too, Mrs MacDonald,' came a Highland voice.

'So ah see, Inspector,' replied Aggie, a smile on her face as she stared at the large wet patch on his uniform. As he got off the tram Aggie commented to one of her passengers. 'See him, talks a loada mince, he does! Never held a wean, Huh! And here's me jist loves weans.'

71

But Aggie's love of children only lasted 24 hours. The following afternoon a wee boy was making a right nuisance of himself. He ran about the lower saloon deck, knocking off hats and making faces at passengers. His mother looked on, every so often giving him a mild, ineffectual rebuke. As Aggie came down the stairs the mother caught the clippie's eye and confided, 'Ah cannae dae oanythin' wi' him. He'll jist no' dae as he's tellt. Makes a right cod o' me he does.'

'Don't worry, hen. Perhaps ah can help.' Aggie moved up the aisle to where the boy was sticking his tongue out at an old lady, bent over and whispered in his ear. Immediately the child ran back to his mother and sat beside her, good as gold.

'Thanks very much,' exclaimed the grateful mother. 'But hoo did ye cure him?'

'Easy, hen. Ah jist telt him that if he didnae behave himsel' ah'd break his bleedin' neck!'

TRAMLINES

The wifie with the messages was inclined to chat as the tram trundled along London Road.

'Ah think you're puttin' oan the beef, Aggie. Yer backside's fair growin'.'

'Listen, you,' countered Aggie. 'Yer givin' ma fat erse a headache. Anyway, yer ain bahookie's jist aboot takin up two seats. Ye should really be buyin' two tickets.'

✳　　✳　　✳

The well-dressed, middle-aged lady sat sobbing on a Kelvinside tram.

'Are ye OK, hen,' enquired Aggie.

The accent was somewhat "pan loaf". 'I am just having a little bubble. I lost my spouse three months ago. He's the third husband I've lost, you know.'

'Loast three husbands!' said Aggie incredulously. 'Jings, yer either awfa lucky or awfa careless.'

*   *   *

Dogs were only allowed on the upper deck of the trams. There was a strict rule that only one dog was allowed to travel on any one tram. (Apart from guide dogs.) Greyhounds were a regular sight on the Carntyne and Shawfield routes.

One day a lady from Newton Mearns sat upstairs with her poodle on her lap. It had just been cut and coiffeured.

She looked up as Aggie quizzically gaped at the dog. 'It's a French poodle, you know.'

'Oh, my. Does it bark in French, then?'

*   *   *

The young woman passenger was obviously very pregnant. As it was mid-morning the tram was relatively quiet. Aggie sat down beside her. 'Thought o' a name yet, hen?' enquired Big Aggie.

'Well, if it's a boy we thought o' callin' him Wullie.'

'Oh, fur heaven's sake,' retorted Aggie. 'Every Tom, Dick and Harry is called Wullie nooadays!'

*   *   *

73

Big Aggie loved babies.

One morning, sitting on the lower saloon with a young child in her arms, sat a stout, young woman.

As she was taking her fare Aggie enquired. 'Is it talkin' yet?'

'Aye,' replied the proud mother. And looking down at the child she said, 'say somethin' fur the nice conductress.'

The child looked up at Aggie from angelic blue eyes and said. 'Away an' fart you!'

Aggie was nonplussed. 'Oh, my,' she commented, 'whit a clear speaker.'

❋ ❋ ❋

Two ladies sat on the lower deck of Aggie's tram going to Burnside, and observed her busily taking fares and giving out tickets.

'Dae ye know whatchamacallur?' enquired one lady.

'Ah don't know her tae speak tae. Ah just know her tae talk aboot.'

❋ ❋ ❋

The overweight drunk had just got on the number 31 to Merrylee, and now he sprawled over a couple of seats. He produced a black pipe with a metal cover.

Aggie stood, with a short measure of patience, while he tried to organize himself.

'Sorry, hen,' he wheezed. 'But ah cannae catch ma breath.

'Wi' your breath ye should be thankful.'

❋ ❋ ❋

Regular driver Jimmy was off with a bad cold and his place had been taken by Ali, a Pakistani. One day, as the tram sat at the terminus at Blairdarie, a wee man stuck his head into the rear platform and asked, 'Hey, does this caur go to the Coo-caddens?'

'It sure does,' replied Aggie.

Aggie then watched him up walk up the outside of the tram, and heard as he asked Ali the very same question. Then, apparently satisfied, he made his way back to the rear platform and boarded the tram.

Aggie gave him a look. 'That you satisfied noo ye've goat it in black and white?'

* * *

The cheeky wee nyaff remonstrated with Aggie as she carefully checked the coins he had handed over for his fare.

'Ah don't think you trust me, Missis, the way yer busy countin' ma ticket money.'

Aggie gave him a withering look.

'Listen, you. Ah never trust oany man wi' short legs. Their brains are too near their erse!'

* * *

The late-night caur was almost full inside. However the only occupants upstairs were three very drunk Glaswegians.

As the tram hurtled down the slope from Cross Stobs it swayed alarmingly from side to side. Screams were heard from the upper deck.

Aggie ran up the stairs and bellowed. 'Whit's goin' oan here? Whit's this screamin'? The folks doonstairs are aw behavin' themselves!'

'Aye,' slurred one of the white-faced drunks, 'but they've goat a driver.'

* * *

The tiny woman had a huge alsatian with her as she tried to board the number 26 tram to Farme Cross.

Aggie was quickly on the scene. 'Naw,' she stated, 'yer dug's too big. It canny cummoan.'

The wee woman protested. 'But ma dug is like wan o' the family.'

'Really! Which wan?'

* * *

The young lassie sat on the top deck of the 29 from Maryhill to Broomhouse. Her legs were crossed and she puffed on a long cigarette.

'This you away tae the Denny Pally tae get yersel' a man?' enquired Aggie as she took her fare.

The reply was indignant. 'A'll huv ye know I've been asked tae get merrit loads o' times.'

'Who asked ye?' came Aggie's reply. 'Yer mither?'

✳   ✳   ✳

A businessman, in bowler hat and pin-stripes, was sitting on Aggie's tram at George Square opposite a harassed wee woman who had her wee boy sitting beside her. The child kept on giving long, noisy sniffs. When Aggie came to take the businessman's fare he remarked, in a somewhat annoyed way, 'Has that boy not got a hankie?'

'Probably he has,' came Aggie's reply. 'But he's no' lendin' it tae you!'

'You're looking gey pleased wi' yersel' the day, Aggie,' observed her driver, Jimmy Tamson, at the start of their shift.

'Ah jist goat back fae a pleasure trip.'

'Where did ye go?'

'Ah wis seein' ma man aff at the Central Station. He's away tae visit his brither in Aiberdeen.'

* * *

The busy number 12 to Mount Florida reached the stop round the corner from a school, and a pile of schoolchildren noisily got off.

A regular passenger turned to Aggie and observed. 'Sure the weans nooadays are gettin' awfa cheeky, Aggie?'

'Yer right,' agreed Big Aggie. 'If ma granny wis alive the day she'd be turnin' in her grave.'

* * *

The fit looking young man with the grumpy face jumped onto Aggie's tram and demanded, 'Hoo much tae Tollcross?'

'Fourpence,' Aggie replied.

'That's far tae dear!' he responded and jumped down off the tram and proceeded to run behind it. A couple of miles further on, he jumped back on the tram, sat down panting and asked, 'Hoo much is it noo?'

'Sixpence.'

'Sixpence!'

'Aye. Ye've been runnin' the wrang way!'

* * *

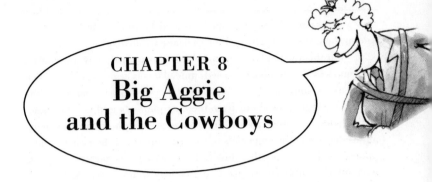

CHAPTER 8
Big Aggie and the Cowboys

THE HEAVY SHOWER came raging up the Clyde, swift and unforgiving, quickly filling the gutters in the canyons of grey tenements with galloping torrents. People tried to take shelter as best they could, standing in shop doorways, muttering about the grey ceiling above and the downpour it was producing. Winter was closing in.

A large Austin motorcar overtook Aggie's tram on the nearside and splashed passengers waiting on the Gallowgate for the number 29 tram to Uddingston. Aggie sympathised with her embarking passengers. 'It's diabolical, that's whit it is. They big motors should be mair careful. Look at you, hen,' she addressed a woman who had taken the brunt of the water and whose dress was now soaked. 'Yer fair wringing. Ye'd better get hame as quick as ye can afore ye get a chill.' Then once more putting on her commanding voice, shouted to the joining passengers. 'Hurry up, pal-eeze! We're a bit behind oor time the day, folks.'

The passengers embarking onto Aggie's tram were the usual combination of an afternoon. Housewives who had been away getting something for their man's tea, a few unemployed men out looking for work, tradesmen going to a job, and a man, a regular passenger, who had no arms.

It seemed that every time Aggie was on this route the 'man with no arms' used her tram. Well into his sixties, tall with a sad face, except when he had been imbibing. Then he was liable to break out into song. 'Home, home on the Range, where the deer and the antelope play,' was his favourite when he had overindulged. Aggie had once asked, 'Hey, did you ever work oan a ranch?' 'Naw, hen, ah jist worked wi' horses in the First World War. That's when ah loast ma arms.' What was unusual about him was that he had no artificial arms, the jacket sleeves hanging limp and empty.

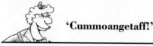

As usual she waited until he seated himself in the busy lower saloon, before ringing the bell for the caur to move off.

On this particular occasion Aggie was immediately aware that the tram was slow to pick up speed, indeed it was crawling along. Then she heard Jimmy use his horn, and strong language came from the front cab. Aggie peered out from the rear platform and saw the cause of the hold up. It was a horse and coal cart. They were forever being a nuisance using the tram rails to ease the burden of their Clydesdales pulling loads over rough cobbles. It appeared this carter was being particularly stubborn, refusing to give way to the tram. As the cart went along the coalman's powerful bass voice boomed out, 'Caw-aw-aw-aw-awl!'

It was quite a while before his red coal cart moved aside and the tram, now well behind schedule, was able to move at a more normal speed.

As the tram finally stopped at Tollcross Park, who appeared but Inspector Campell, watch in hand.

'You're three minutes late, Motorman Tamson.' he pronounced solemnly to Jimmy. 'That's an offence which carries a two-day suspension, you know.'

'Sorry, Inspector, but ah wis held up by wan o' they carters running his cairt wheels alang the rails.'

'So he wis, Inspector,' came the voice of Big Aggie. 'It wis yon coalman wi' the red cairt. He's a right bandit.'

'You're driver should take the appropriate action, Mrs MacDonald. Use the horn, and if necessary inform the police. I'm going to let you off this time, but next time ... 'He let the threat hang in the air.

After the inspector departed Jimmy was concerned. 'Whit am ah gonny dae. Yon coalman'll no let me past. He'll get me suspended and ah'll lose pay.'

'Don't ye worry, Jimmy, ah'll fix it,' reassured Aggie.

But it happened again the very next day at exactly the same time. There, ahead of them, was the same red coal cart. Jimmy again used the horn, loud and long, but was ignored by the carter.

'That's it! Wur no' havin' this nonsense,' exclaimed Aggie. She immediately ran up the stairs to the upper deck, made her way to the front, pulled on the strap to open the window above the destination board, and to the amusement of her intrigued passengers yelled. 'Hey,

Roy Rogers!' She saw the carter turn his head and look up at the source of the shout. 'Mmm,' she thought, 'no' a bad lookin' big fella.' Then bawling at the top of her voice yelled, 'Get you an Trigger aff oor rails. Errapolis behind this caur!'

The carter immediately gave the Clydesdale a clip with his long whip, pulled on the reins, and the red cart containing coal and briquettes swung over to the left.

Aggie closed the window and swiftly made her way downstairs to the rear platform, just as the tram passed the cart.

'Where's the polis, then?' the carter shouted at her, his handsome, dirty face turning red.

'Two miles back in the Sheriff's office at the Tron.' And she gave him a cheery wave, blew a kiss, raising her skirt a couple of inches. He suddenly smiled, and blew a kiss back. Aggie turned into the lower saloon. 'Ah think yon cowboy fancies me,' she observed to the passengers nearest the platform, before moving into the lower saloon. 'Ferrs, pal-leeze. Huv yer money ready.'

A wee man in the second seat had a cunning look in his eye as he looked up at the approaching Aggie. 'Hey, big yin,' he said. 'Am black-affronted. Ah seem tae huv left ma money at hame.'

Aggie's eye glinted. 'Well, wee yin. Ah'm black-hearted. Aff, ya wee nyaff.' Aggie rang the bell and the caur stopped. The man got off. Once safely on the pavement he turned and used a few choice words, but Aggie was already taking more fares.

As she busied herself up the now swaying car, she came to 'the man with no arms'. She knew that as usual his money would be in the top pocket of his jacket. He greeted her with a familiar smile and as he did so, she noticed he had a cold with snot on his upper lip. Aggie took the change from his pocket and said as she did so. 'A four-penny one, isn't it?' He nodded. She produced the ticket from her machine and stuck it in his pocket. As she did so Aggie produced a handkerchief from her uniform, and with the dexterity of a conjurer ordered, 'Blow!' The handkerchief quickly disappeared, and from another pocket came a mint imperial which she stuck into his mouth. In a flash she was onto the next passenger before quickly moving through the rest of the caur.

An elderly lady sitting on the seat behind the 'man with no arms', turned with a tear in her eye to her companion. 'Did ye see yon, Jessie. Hard as nails wan minute an' an angel the next. Could only happen in Glesca.'

Every day thereafter when Aggie's tram came up behind 'Roy Rogers' and his red coal cart, a couple of hoots on the horn did the trick and the carter let them passed. Aggie made a point of giving him a wave and blowing a kiss.

'Works every time,' said Aggie to Jimmy.

'Ah think you fancy that big Roy Rogers,' observed Jimmy.

'Ah'm saying nothing till ah see ma lawyer,' smiled Aggie.

A couple of days later Aggie's early evening tram was full of dancers going to Barrowland. As they left the tram one girl turned to Aggie. 'No' fancy goin' fur a dance, Aggie? It's somebuddy called somethin' like Geraldo or Geronimo that's oan the night.'

'Naw,' replied Aggie, 'ah prefer the cowboys tae the Injuns.'

TRAMLINES ...
THE END OF THE LINE

The spiv with his teddy boy suit and winklepicker shoes sat admiring his reflection in the tram window. He ran a comb through the Brylcreemed hair. Suddenly he looked up, conscious that Aggie had been standing watching him.

'Ah'm gettin' a divorce,' he blurted out.

'Oh, aye. Who's the lucky wumman, then?'

✳   ✳   ✳

One day, Aggie's cousin's boy was a passenger on her tram. A lazy lad, he looked even more unhappy than usual.

Aggie's greeting to him was, 'Hey, Peter, yer face is fair trippin' ye. Does that mean you've goat a job?'

He looked at her sheepishly. 'Ah've goat a job at the sewage works doon in Govan.'

'Huh! Knowin' you, you'll just be goin' through the motions!'

On a number 25 bound for Springburn, Big Aggie reproached a young man for his lack of manners, not standing to give his seat to a middle-aged lady.

'Right you. Up!' The young man saw the glint of steel in her eye and wisely stood up and gave way.

Turning to the woman, Aggie instructed. 'Noo, hen, jist you plank yer weary erse oan that seat.'

* * *

'Ah'm awfa sorry, Missis,' said a woman passenger to Aggie one morning as the conductress was collecting fares. 'But ma wee boy has eaten oor tickets. Whit am ah goin' tae dae?'

'Hoo aboot buying a second helping!'

* * *

The tram was stationary at a fare stage on Argyle Street, all the fares had been collected. Aggie was standing on the rear platform looking out at the crowds of people thronging the pavements. A foreign-looking chap stuck his head in the rear platform and enquired of Aggie.

'Parlez-vous Francais?'

Getting no reply he tried again.

'Habla Espagnol?'

With no answer forthcoming he then asked, 'Sprechen sie Deutsch?'

Giving up, he disappeared into the crowd of pedestrians. A passenger sitting near the platform commented to Aggie. 'Dae ye think, Aggie, it wid no' be a good idea if, in Scotland, we wur aw tae learn mair than wan language?'

The reply was quick. 'Didnae dae him oany good, did it?'

* * *

The young lady from Bearsden was dressed to the 'nines'. She saw Aggie eyeing her finery as the clippie took the fare.

'I'm going shopping in Buchanan Street for my "going away" suit,' she informed Aggie. Then she added. 'I tell you, conductress. A whole lot of men are going to be miserable when I marry.'

Aggie just couldn't resist it. 'Hoo many men are ye going tae marry, then?'

* * *

The leisurely moving number 14 to Kelvingrove was almost empty, and Aggie was passing the time chatting away to a passenger.

'Whit kind o' family did ye come frae, Aggie?'

'Nuthin' special. We wur poor but dishonest.'

* * *

A lady with the blue rinse, fur stole, fur coat and fur hat squeezed her bulky way past Aggie and, in a somewhat flamboyant manner, took her seat in the lower-deck saloon. The high-stepper then made a great display of opening her matching handbag, producing a gold powder compact and applying make-up.

Aggie, along with most of the passengers, watched this performance. Aggie gave a knowing wink at a couple of her regular passengers and observed.

'Sure it's great whit ye see when you huvnae goat a gun!'

Aggie thought she recognised the male traveller. Could he be a Glesca Corporation cooncillur? she wondered. When she asked him for his fare it was clear he hadn't any money ready in his hand. 'Do you know who I am?' he demanded haughtily.

'When did ye lose yer memory, then?'

    ✱   ✱   ✱

The young lady on the lower deck was dressed ready for the jigging at the Albert Ballroom. However, the dance dress she was wearing was, to put it mildly, rather revealing at the front.

'Whit dae ye think o' ma new outfit, Aggie?' she enquired.

Aggie gave her one look and observed. 'Ye've goat a cleavage on ye like a sheep's heid!'

    ✱   ✱   ✱

A coal cart pulled by a large Clydesdale horse was standing beside the pavement as Aggie's tram drew up. The coalman was clearly lost and shouted into the tram. 'Can oanybuddy tell me where MacIntyre's coal yard is roon here?'

Tram Inspector Campbell, standing on the rear platform checking Aggie's ticket machine, shouted out.

'Ah, yes, my good man. Traverse at right angles, pass through a single arch and an edifice will become readily acceptable to your ocular senses. There you may evacuate the contents of your vehicle.'

The coalman's mouth hung open as he tried to comprehend the

instructions. However Aggie came to his rescue.

'It's through that gate across the street!' she shouted. And then as an aside to one of her passengers stated. 'Sure it's diabolical. Yon cannae speak right. Did ye ever hear such a loada mince!'

*　　*　　*

It was the terminus at Burnside, and just as the tram stopped, Aggie, on the rear platform, slipped from the tram.

A concerned passenger enquired, 'Are ye hurtit, Aggie?'

'Naw 'am fine,' she replied. 'Ah wis gettin' aff oanway.'

*　　*　　*

The tram was running late one winter's evening and, as it shoogled away from a Fare Stop in Maxwell Road, a red-faced fellow came running up. Aggie knew him ... he had given her hassle in the past.

'Haud up yer tram, conductress!' he shouted after the vehicle now disappearing in the thin yellow light from the street lamps.

'Sorry, pal,' Aggie boomed back. 'It's too heavy!'

*　　*　　*

The early morning tram had just started off from the Fare Stage at Springfield Road. A passenger was just about to clatter up the stairs when he heard Big Aggie's tired voice boom out.

'Doon inside here fur oany sake. Ah huvnae had time tae get upstairs an' there's no' a bed made yet!'

*　　*　　*

The two stoney-faced sisters sat together downstairs every morning on Aggie's tram. They continually followed Aggie's every move in a critical frosty-eyed silence. Finally Aggie could stand it no longer and the next day as she collected their fares, remarked, 'Huv you two come oot again an' left Cinders in hersel'?'